N TERRITORY of AUSTRALIA
134°
135°
136°
ARAFURA SEA
Goulburn I
Goulburn Is
Cape Stewart
CROCODILE Is
ELCHO I.
WESSEL ISLANDS
Boucaut Bay
Maningrida
MILINGIMBI
Mission
HOWARD I.
Buckingham Bay
ARNHEM BAY
Melville Bay
YIRRKALA
GOVE
Cape Arnhem
12°
Liverpool R.
CADELL R.
ARAFURA SWAMP
Mitchell Ranges
Port Bradshaw
ARNHEM
LAND
CALEDON BAY
Cape Grey
13°
Cape Shield
BLUE MUD BAY
WILTON RIVER
Mission
GROOTE EYLANDT
14°
Rose River
Rose River Mission
Tasman Pt
GULF OF CARPENTARIA
ROPER RIVER
Port Roper
15°

Frank Hodgkinson's

Kakadu and the Arnhem Landers

Frank Hodgkinson's

Kakadu

and the

Arnhem Landers

WELDONS

*for Kate —
her belief
and research
are central
to the work*

Published by Weldons Pty Ltd
43 Victoria Street
McMahons Point NSW 2060 Australia
A member of the Weldon-Hardie Group of Companies
Sydney . Auckland . Hong Kong . London . Chicago

Jacket Design: Eymont Design

Colour separations by: Rainbow Graphic Arts Co Ltd, Hong Kong
Printed by: Everbest Printing Co Ltd, Hong Kong

National Library of Australia Cataloguing-in-Publication Data
Hodgkinson, Frank, 1919-
Frank Hodgkinson's Kakadu and the Arnhem landers.

ISBN 0 947116 43 5.

1. Hodgkinson, Frank, 1919- – Views on Kakadu National Park (N.T.) 2. Hodgkinson, Frank, 1919- – Views on Aborigines, Australian. 3. Painting, Australian – Northern Territory – Kakadu National Park. 4. Aborigines, Australian – Northern Territory – Kakadu National Park. 5. Aborigines, Australian in art – Northern Territory – Kakadu National Park. I. Title.

994.29'450049915

A KEVIN WELDON PRODUCTION

Contents

Foreword	7
Introduction	11
Bathurst and Melville Islands	17
Cobourg Peninsula	37
Burrunguy (Nourlangie Rock)	63
Oenpelli and Ubirr (Obiri Rock)	127
Deaf Adder Gorge, Jim Jim and Bilk Bilkmi	185
Goulburn Islands	223
Gove Peninsula	243

Foreword

Frank Hodgkinson must have spent more time working as an artist in Arnhem Land than any other acknowledged Australian artist. I have lost count of the number of times he has sallied forth on his own, with his wife Kate or, more often over the last seven years, as a regular member of the Northern Territory Museum's annual Artists' Camp.

What is so remarkable about Frank's approach to Arnhem Land, apart from his ability, inspiration, artistry and brilliance as a draftsman, is the prodigious amount of work he has produced and, more particularly, the incredible depth of personal involvement he has demonstrated. Not for him the changing landscape alone as a source of realism, impressionism or abstraction! The totality is his inspiration. This has required an obsessive interest in the people, particularly Aboriginal, with their ancient and varied legends, rituals and artforms, in the natural history, the geology and the meteorology of the area. Everything is a source of inspiration. His research has required effort to the level of exhaustion, as it can, indeed, be exhausting for those he questions. The result is both chronicle and art worthy of a Renaissance man.

This book reveals, I believe, a development upon Hodgkinson's previous book, *Sepik Diary*, with which it obviously has a commonality of purpose. More importantly, it reflects Frank's fascination with and personal involvement in wilderness and its inhabitants, human and other.

It has been a very great delight and inspiration for me to have been associated in some small way with Frank's production of this most splendid work, and I respectfully but heartily commend it to the reader.

Dr Colin Jack-Hinton
Director
Museums and Art Galleries of the Northern Territory

10 | V
to Darwin 19 | 78

Introduction

Two thousand million years of
experience secreted in that
escarpment, say archeologists.
A concept too vast to grasp.
Perhaps here, long before man, life began.
Like the empty sky this
landscape has no boundaries.
And things in it, not previously seen,
are familiar, like images long forgotten —
archetypal images found in child art,
that of the Bushmen of South Africa,
the Palaeolithic cave art of Europe and
recent paintings by Dubuffet, Miro et al.
Images that split the sequence of time —
time without tense.
Life is a collection of moments. Some
moments, not always in sequence,
from experiences on seven years
of journeys into Arnhem Land
are collected here.

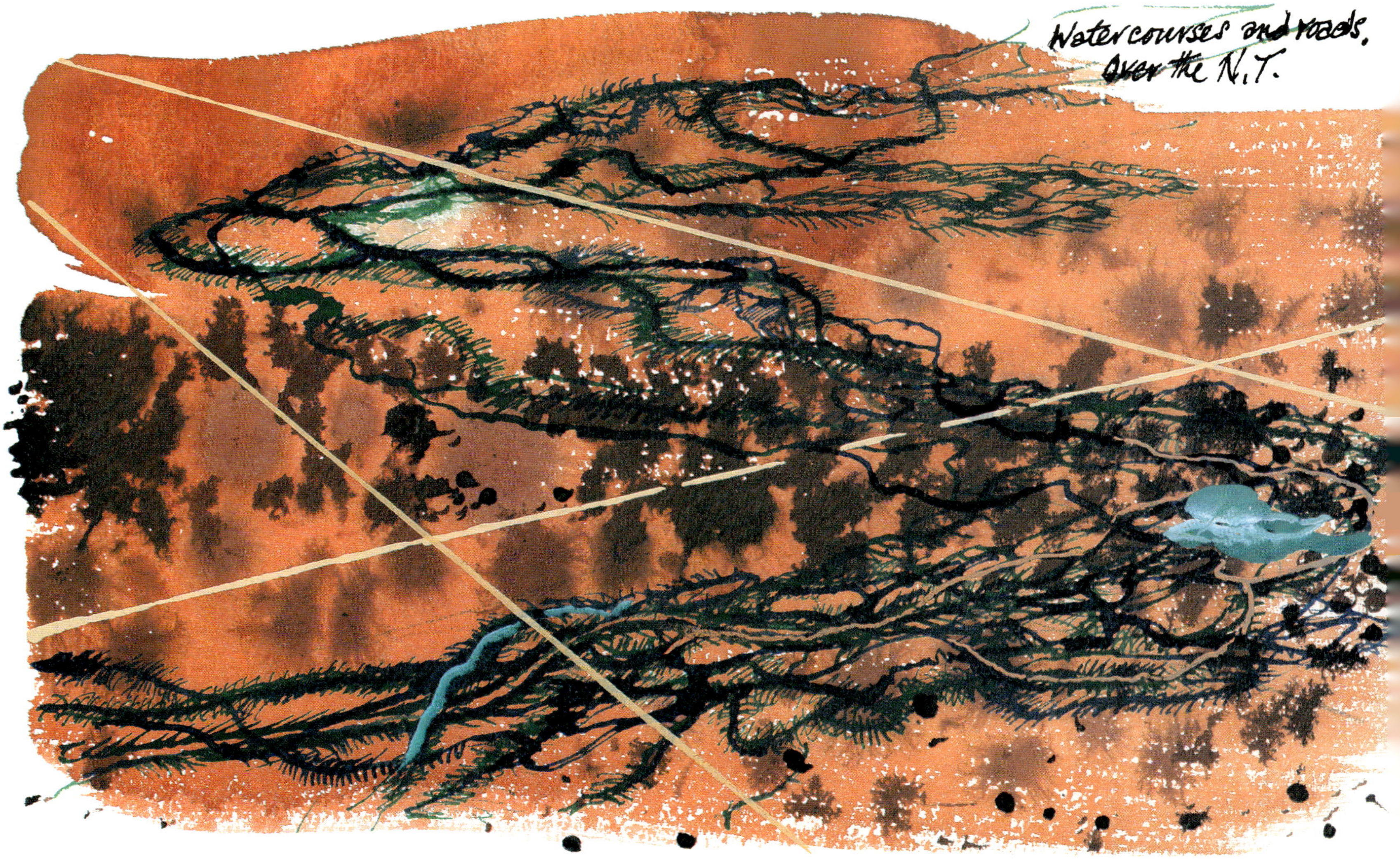

Millipede lines, emerald and olive in tangled frenzy on red-ochre ground— tree banked river beds stilled in the dry map the urgent passage of the wet's flooding, criss-crossing yet concerted in direction like the trails of foraging ants. Concepts flood the vision above five thousand metres. Closer to earth the mind recalls the likeness of things seen in normal perspective. Flying high the spirit is free, the mind liberated, space is limitless.

A similar sense of space is enjoyed by

Aborigines. It is expressed in most of their art forms, particularly in paintings on bark. Their "sky" concept of spatial relationships reflects their semi-nomadic existence — the Aborigine is rarely confined within four walls. His space is contained by the universe, his nocturnal ceiling a sparkling vastness.

Relatively, Western art space is enclosed, cosily domesticated and framed by an inward-looking metropolitan way of life.

Environment controls the separate ways of seeing. In painting a still-life of food the Western artist is detached from the subject. The vegetables, fruit or fish are simply objects to be placed

A map of water courses. From a bark painting of the Rembarnga, Maningrida

within a given space for aesthetic reasons. The Aboriginal artist's concept of a similar subject is totally involved in food as the essence of body and soul. Homage is paid to ancestor beings who created the food source, who planted the original yams and brought the

barramundi from the sea into the freshwater billabongs of Western Arnhem Land, thus providing plentifully for the Gunwinggu people. Totems and images of hunting and fishing magic are painted to ensure success.

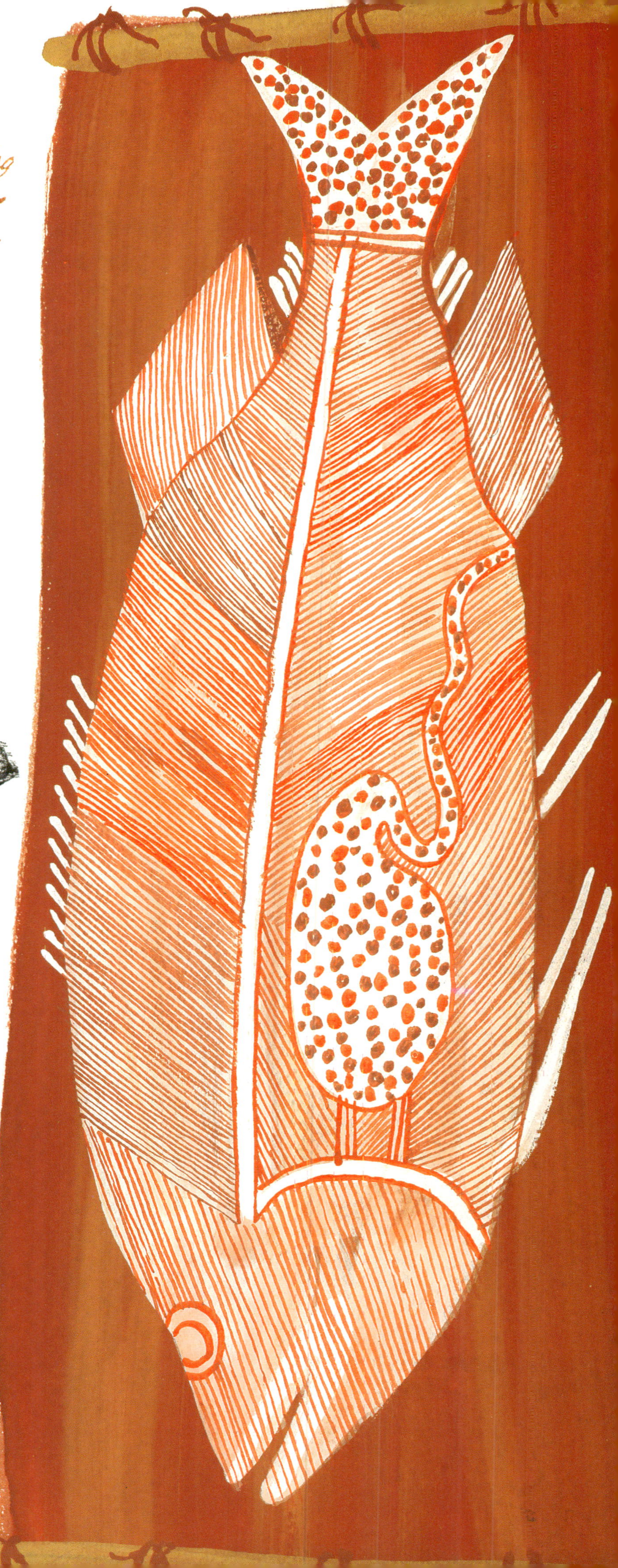

from a bark painting of the Gunwinggu. Oenpelli.

Bathurst and Melville Islands –
In the first attempt to settle the north British troops at Fort Dundas found the Tiwi aggressive in defence of their islands.
To this day the Tiwi observe the ritual of their traditional hunter-gatherer lifestyle.
In a highly structured patriarchal society they celebrate death in elaborate Pukumani ceremonies.

It could have been paradise and no doubt it was a short time ago. Fibro and iron shanties, junked cars and the inevitable glitter of beer cans identify this as another disastrous attempt to bring Aborigines into the twentieth century. This is bush holiday time the schools are closed. Many families camp by the dusty roadside rather than on the beach so the men can hitch a ride to the settlement and collect their beer ration of six cans a day.

In a twin engined Cessna it had been a short thirty minutes across Beagle Gulf from Darwin to Snake Bay on Melville Island. About the same stretch of water that separates England from France but for thousands of years the gulf had been fixed. There had been no contact between mainland Aborigines and the Tiwi of Melville and Bathurst Islands. On a cloudless day the Tiwi had a hazy view of the mainland coast, a land they called Tibambinumi, home of the dead, a final resting place for their spirits. Existence beyond their islands was inconceivable for the Tiwi, 'we the people', who had no word for 'others'.

Running behind time after picking me up at the airstrip Jim is pushing the truck hard over the dirt. Many camps by the side of the road are happily colourful. Awnings draped from saplings and women's dresses with traditional patterns, printed at Cottage Crafts on Bathurst Island, appear freshly laundered. A young girl kicks dust at a dog reluctant to get off the road and an old man squatting on a mound of bulldozed red soil signals us to stop. As the truck grinds to a standstill its dust engulfs us and a young Tiwi approaches slowly to complain about a burst inner-tube. Though now officer-in-charge of Forestry, Jim Weston, essentially a kind man, had been a mechanic and it seems the entire community still relies upon him to keep their wheels turning.

At home on the waterfront of Snake Bay set among

well tended lawns, palms and orchids Jim offers me the choice of an apartment where I could spread my painting materials or staying in the house. I accept their hospitality when his wife Anne points out the hazards of shopping and cooking and Jim offers studio space in his office. In a later aside Jim explains had I opted for the apartment he would have warned that girls might proposition me for cash which they would give to their men waiting on the beach who would then pester me with demands for grog.

The good Father Gsell and his French nuns who had established a mission in 1911 at Paru on Melville clearly had failed in an effort to evangelise the Tiwi. Buffalo shooter Joe Cooper, then virtual king of Melville, had warned Gsell of the Tiwis' resentment of intruders. They had lived in splendid isolation fiercely rebuffing the Malays and an early European bid to settle. Cooper's original efforts to dig in had been violently uprooted. He had retreated to Port Essington taking with him four captive Tiwis whom he treated well. Before returning to Melville Island he put the four once captive Tiwis ashore to spread the message of his beneficence towards them. His second attempt to settle was unmolested. With him travelled an entourage of Port Essington Aborigines including his wife who shadowed him as constant body guard.

Blue-black and powerfully built the Tiwi had a unique social system which exploited the islands' abundant and varied food sources. The gathering of fruit, vegetables, grubs and fish was done by women and children. The more important the patriarch the more wives he could have and many wives meant full bellies. Sons and stepsons hunted animals while the patriarch himself spent his days in the development of dance choreography, song cycles, the carving and decoration of magnificent ceremonial spears — the visible evidence of his personal wealth and standing in the community. Such a man of status would sling six or more spears over his shoulder.

The double-barbed spear, Tjunkuletti, used in ceremonies such as Pukamani is cut out of one solid piece of timber. Various woods are used, the very heavy hard ironwood erythrophleum chlorostachys was preferred, carved with Cyrena shell.

One of the most commonly seen of ceremonial Tiwi spears. Length 3,000mm. The design is frequently found on painted clubs and on body decoration, the reds, yellows and whites alternating. Below the barbs string is wound, covered with beeswax and whitened. Appears the head has been hafted onto the shaft.

Most decorative type of all ceremonial spears. Measuring at their widest 470mm. The five barbs (double) are carved in perfect symmetry, the dividing cuts extremely fine. The pattern on each barb is imaginatively varied and delicately painted. The shaft is ornamented with Abrus seeds fixed with beeswax and painted.

Another variation in carved and decorated Tiwi spears. Below its ten double-barbs the blade has been honed down flat and opened to a square hole. None of the Tiwi spears has the little cavity in the tip of the shaft to fit into the point of a woomera. Though spear-throwers are used by mainland tribes as near as the Iwaidja on the Cobourg Peninsula they are unknown on Bathurst and Melville Islands.

Female ceremonial spear — a form rarely seen. Length 2620mm, blade 1060mm. Carved from a solid piece of ironwood by 'Frog' Wokkatamini (died 1972), regarded by the Tiwi as the best spearmaker on Bathurst Island — probably the last of the great craftsmen because today much smaller spears are made from light timbers.

Of simpler design this spear has two holes (which suggest eyes) pierced and circled with red-ochre below the barbs.
Across the vast continent from Tasmania to the Northern Territory there is little variation in types and design of spears. Cape Don on the Cobourg Peninsula is just 25 kms across Dundas Strait from Melville Island yet the Iwaidja on the peninsula have none of the Tiwi's widely varied spears and the Islanders have ignored those from the mainland.

Male ceremonial spear — length overall 2250 mm., blade 720mm. Carved by 'Black Jack' Wombi-au-dimirra who lived at Snake Bay and died in 1974. Black Jack's craftsmanship is celebrated widely as the greatest from Melville Island.

Distinct from other types of decorative spears, either on the islands or on the mainland, these intricately patterned examples such as the 'female' the one above and that second from the top, are the least common among the Tiwi. The formidable time necessary to carve and paint the complicated designs and the very few talented artists along with an increasing loss of dedication have made these spears collectors' pieces.

One of the longest spears — overall 4,094 mm., blade 1520mm., width 70mm.

he creative talents
certain patriachs
vere more fruitfully
ployed in dance than
the making of spears.
rom a careful study
an emu and her
——— chicks dance
routines evolved.

Tiwi youths decorated
as emu chicks mime
the fledglings' frustrated
attempts to fly.

Spiritual rather than physical penetration was believed to cause pregnancy but to avoid illegitimacy no woman could be husbandless at any time from birth to death. Infant girls were betrothed to men of advanced years who could be seventy or more when the bride reached puberty. Bestowal of the female was vested on her father or stepfather and he used his commodity to his own good advantage. Older widows of strong personality at times demanded the right to choose a husband among younger men who could not expect a nubile in residence till achieving forty or more summers. As each family unit was self-contained these older women ensured a supply of food and their experience helped indoctrinate the influx of younger wives. As moral guardians the old ones kept an eye on young wives inclined to dalliance with young men while foraging for food, the cause of many arguments around the camp fire.

In a practical effort to reform the Tiwi and enable girls to choose their male partners Father Gsell himself entered the marriage market. With commodities such as tobacco, flour, cloth, axes and trinkets he purchased widowed infant girls from their fathers. In unconsummated wedlock he had many, many wives. Wild stories of this well-meaning priest appeared in newspapers of the southern states and in later years when he was Bishop of Darwin he was dubbed the Bishop with one hundred and fifty wives. To commemorate Father Gsell's courageous though somewhat futile crusade a small stone effigy, stark white and elevated on a pedestal, European in concept and incongruous in this setting keeps an eye on Bathurst Island over Apsley Strait from the old mission at Paru.

After World War I Japanese pearlers working off-shore waters competed in this barter for young girls and with superior resources paid off the fathers, husbands and brothers who had control of them. In 1940 a new Roman Catholic mission was established at Garden Point to care for and educate half caste children.

This social system which reduced women to a form

of capital asset to be manipulated by men during their lifetime returned them in death equal burial rites. And the exuberant Tiwis' complex ceremonial life is dominated by the passage of the spirit of the dead through ritual known as Pukumani, a ceremony completed in stages over a long period. Rituals for revered men would continue for years. Close relatives of the deceased may not participate in preparation for mortuary ceremonies. Said to be in a state of Pukumani (dangerous or set apart) they may not touch food and are fed by others. Distant relatives make decorative baskets and commission the carving of burial posts known as Pukumani poles — these at the instruction of the mythical Purukupali. Some distance from the camp the corpse was interred, the grave covered with a sheet of paper-bark, the surrounding grass and scrub cleared. The site was undisturbed for two months when the first of three ceremonies, performed over as many months, commenced. The ritual acts or Ilania for which faces and bodies were carefully decorated, the women holding large woven armlets close to their bodies to prevent them slipping, were danced in the smoke of a fire to disguise any personal smell the spirit might recognise. Men danced into and leapt over the fire to singe their legs. A month later the second Ilania, similar in make-up and dance, stages the ritual feeding of the pole-makers

Bathurst Is. Pukumani pole.
Carved from single trunk of ironwood.
Dug up in 1975 after ceremonies and retouched

and a fight between these and the mourners. Further diversion is provided by married men and women who strip branches from trees to flay their in-laws. Finally condolences in the form of message sticks are dispatched to far flung relatives.

The five part final ceremony is celebrated over several days. These are similar in form to the initial Ilanias though pole-makers are paid in the third when gourds or baskets are placed on the poles. The poles are carried to the grave in the fourth and erected. In the fifth and final act the grave is cleared of its cover of bushes and wailing mourners prostrate themselves over the mound. Beards of the chief mourners are plucked and body decoration is washed off — a painful operation for this old chap, his whiskers set in the sap of a milk-wood tree to give him the electrified look of a bearded dragon.

Inquests are customary. After the burial medicine men investigate the ground around the grave, examine the track of an animal, a bird which frequents the site, a suspicious hole. Some guilty being or scapegoat must be found. In the case of a witnessed killing the culprit may be proven to be the unwitting agent of sorcery. Revenge is not always desirable; knowing the guilty party may be satisfaction enough.

Today at Snake Bay pukumani poles still rise like sentinels watching over Beagle Gulf to the land of the dead but rusty iron replaces the fresh sheet of paper-bark and rather than highly personal items, a lock of hair and a finger bone in a dillybag or a superbly crafted spear, a broken transistor and a burnt-out electric stove are tossed on to the grave. Beside a corrugated iron grave at another burial ground, where termites are reducing the pukumani posts to dust, there is a simple and unmarked mound covered with a child's sheet patterned with Disneyland images — Mickey Mouse in a ten gallon hat.

Snake Bay, Melville Island.
A dramatic enacting of an incident in the life of the deceased during a Pukumani ceremony.

Large decorated bark basket contains food for those who made the mortuary Posts and baskets
Headdress of White cockatoo feathers

Tiwi girl decorated and wearing armlets for pukumani ceremony. Painted wood carving with bark skirt. Bathurst Island.

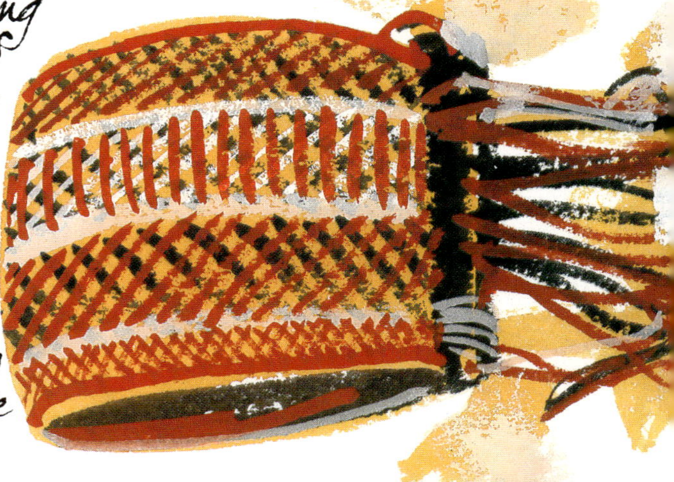

Armlets worn at pukumani mourning ceremonies Made from the bark of the Stringy-bark eucalypt and painted in ochres white and black Abrus seeds stuck with beeswax to a stick is passed through the centre

Decorated discs carried by women at pukumani ceremony
above decoration suggests rigging of a sailing ship.
Nankeen night-heron feathers
split cockatoo and brown owl feathers
Bark basket placed over a pukumani post

Though the Red-tailed Black cockatoo is more appropriately adorned for mortuary ceremony it is, in fact, the White (opposite) which appears in Tiwi ritual.

Also known as the Banksian it was the first Australian cockatoo to be drawn by a European — Sydney Parkinson illustrator to Joseph Banks on the 'Endeavour' in 1770.

About 60 cms from crest to tail this magnificent bird nests in tree hollows, chewing away the inside to create a cushion of wood chip on which to lay its solitary egg.

Its raucous, grating screech is deafening when amplified by a couple of hundred birds which would amount to a normal flock.

The White cockatoo's association with Tiwi mortuary ceremony extends beyond the use of its feathers in headdresses. It is believed to keep a sentinal eye on wayward spirits lost en route to the island of the dead. Its imperative call alerts Aborigines to spirits in limbo among the rocks and scrub of Arnhem Land.

Also known as the Sulphur-crested these cockatoos feed on grass seed, budding leaves, nuts and insects and their lavae. A bird or two high in trees warn the feeding flock against predators. For this reason men posted on watch for police around illegal gambling activities such as 'two-up' schools are dubbed cockatoos.

Jostling for sleeping perch in a roosting tree cockatoos screech-up a domestic brawl till long after sunset.

Cobourg Peninsula.

The influence of Macassan trepang fishermen on Aboriginal culture in Arnhem Land is apparent to this day.
— Millions of years of slowly evolved ecology changed abruptly under the impact of water-buffalo introduced through the trading posts of Fort Wellington and Victoria.
— Ludwig Leichhardt's epic overland journey to Port Essington is contrasted with my own voyage under sail.

Heavy rain has flattened and glazed the sea pea-green. "The wind is as faint as an angel's fart," observes Lou as he starts the diesel again, "Under power we generate our own wind. It fills the sails but doesn't help much."

We had climbed aboard at 0830 hours. Colin Jack-Hinton with correct sea-kit and clipper skipper's cap had been appalled by my landlubber's suitcase, "Doubt they'll allow that on board, old chap." The solidly built case contained tubes of paint and a change of clothes; in a canvas kit bag all items would be written off if sat upon.

The ketch, Windfall, with its two masted jauntiness is a glaring red. It had been white but for practical reasons Lou had painted it red; it still gathers slime but now it doesn't show. The ferro-cement hull was constructed for stability on long voyages rather than racing in the twelve metre class. Its power unit, a salvaged 38 h.p. Perkins diesel, was built originally to generate electricity. Later it propelled a large trimaran until wrecked and tossed up on Darwin beach. The timber superstructure was built entirely by the skipper, Lou Marchant; it has been his home since his marriage broke up.

The course is set from Darwin Harbour to Cape Don and the Cobourg Peninsular. Our destination is Port Essington, the site of the early settlement of Victoria, abandoned one hundred and thirty two years ago. The commission is to assess the viability of conserving the ruins of this forsaken outpost of the Empire as a national monument.

Out of Beagle Gulf and through Howard Channel we navigate the Vernons, a group of islands named after Admiral 'Grog' Vernon, a commander not averse to splicing the mainbrace. Our volunteer deck hand, a Darwin crane operator, answers to 'Groggie.' He comments that a ration of rum would ease the monotony of this foreshore. With the sun over the yardarm we break open a carton of beer and lunch on salami, a hot one, bread and salad.

Past Cape Hotham towards Abbott Shoal, Melville and Bathurst Islands appear on the north-western horizon shortly before the darkening sky obscures them.

March flies which trailed and strafed us throughout the day have returned to land for the night. Dead calm at sea and though under power the Windfall's sails refuse to fill even with false wind. Against tide and current little way is made. Sleep under a canopy of brilliant stars is broken by the watches. Each of us takes the helm for a couple of hours, steering directly towards the distant blinks of Cape Don lighthouse which seems no nearer now than it had some hours back.

A trawler flying and plunging its huge steel prawning nets crosses and recrosses our course. The Windfall's mast light has failed so Lou flashes a torch into the mizzen. To further hazard our passage the Cape Don, a fast ship which services lighthouses, manoeuvres close by. Electrical failure now douses the Windfall's navigation lights. Among his souvenirs Lou has a Portuguese flag. Resourcefully he hands the red and green flag and the torch to Groggie who dashes back and forth across the foredeck flashing through the red of the flag to port and through the green to starboard. The Cape Don with its helipad stern gaily lit looks festive, and dolphins swimming alongside, displaying in pairs, are great fun. Lou points out further evidence of their well known intelligence — they never go for lures.

Patches of verdigris and golden plankton float lazily on a deepening sea of azure as we round Cape Don shortly after dawn. Along Cobourg Peninsula the foreshores of Blue Mud and Trepang Bays are fringed with a monotony of mangroves. A strip of frothy white off Vashon Head is a reminder of the many uncharted reefs along the north coast. This one claimed the Orontes which wrecked in 1838, the year prior to John Lort Stokes survey voyage along this coast as Commander of the Beagle.

Stokes was the first European to set foot ashore at Port Darwin, which he named after a young naturalist who had sailed on the Beagle's World Voyage of 1831-36 never dreaming Charles Darwin would become famous.

Enthralled by this coastline Stokes visualised a

great future for British Christian civilisation in the far north of Australia. Alas, before that enthusiast had seen it two attempts at colonisation had failed: Fort Dundas on Melville Island (1824-29) and Fort Wellington at Raffles Bay (1827-29). Motivated by strategy and interest in trade the British Government's policy embraced little Christianity. In the 17th century the Dutch had pushed the British out of the Indonesian Archipelago. War with the French and the Dutch late in the next century together with a flourishing trade with China caused the British to seek new bases near to the East.

Unlike Stokes Phillip King had not been enthusiastic about the Arnhem Land coast he had surveyed, but wrote of Port Essington:

> As a harbour Port Essington is equal if not superior to any I ever saw; and from its proximity to the Moluccas and New Guinea, and its being on the direct line of communication between Port Jackson and India, as well as its commanding situation with respect to the passage through Torres Strait, it must, at no very distant period, become a place of great trade, and of very considerable importance.

Commissioned to establish an outpost there, Capt J.J.G. Bremer, commanding a flotilla of three ships, twenty-six marines and twenty-five troops, paused only three days at Port Essington before sailing on to Melville Island where drinking water was good. A pier was projected into Apsley Strait and on an elevated site Fort Dundas was built inside a stockade of thick timber and a battery of cannons. Local Aborigines were openly hostile to the intruders. The Tiwi tore down huts, speared livestock, stole tools and killed many of the settlers. A soldier disappeared on a bush walk. Dressed in his clothes his wife searched the bush for some sign of him; she was 'wild', said the soldiers who found and brought her back.

As a trading port Fort Dundas failed to attract a single vessel, though hundreds of Macassan praus were known to be collecting trepang along the coast. A second attempt to assert British possession of Northern Australia and to establish another "Singapore" was made three years later at Raffles Bay on the mainland. On a shore of mudbanks and exposed reefs Captain James Stirling chose the site for Fort Wellington. He left the building of it to fourteen marines, thirty soldiers, twenty-two convicts, a Malay interpreter and his son, a surgeon, a storekeeper, two women and five children. Humid heat and hurricanes plagued the colony and destroyed crops. Mud mangroves; mosquitoes, sandflies and fear of black men undermined morale. Poor diet and careless hygiene caused diseases such as dysentery, scurvy, hepatitis and night blindness. Malaria, brought in from Timor by crews of supply ships, killed six of the tiny colony in one week.

Misunderstanding and violent clashes between blacks and whites were finally resolved by the last commandant at Raffles Bay. The example of Captain Collett Barker's personal courage in walking unarmed with Aborigines through the bush to their camps, where he slept at times, spread goodwill far beyond the area. When he first landed on Croker Island he was greeted enthusiastically as 'Commandant.' Morale improved and the Buginese fishermen from Macassar visited. More than a thousand seamen of thirty-four praus came ashore at Fort Wellington between March and May of 1829, the year the British Government ordered the abandonment of the settlement, not long after the closure of Fort Dundas. On the eve of success the settlers were forced to quit; the buildings and fertile gardens were left to the Aborigines. Ten years later French explorer Dumont D'Urville found that the gardens had returned to the bush and the stockade walls were down. Every bit of iron including coffin nails had been removed by Aborigines.

The serenity of the vast sea and sky is accentuated by a translucent light filtering through the Windfall's awning, a necessary screen for our bodies, already glowing from the second day's exposure. At 1530 hours the anchor is dropped off Black Point and we put ashore in a cockle-shell of a dinghy. Seven aluminium runabouts are pulled up on the sandy beach, which is protected by a reef, and moored offshore is the ranger's landing barge, the Britomart, named after the barque that was painted by Owen Stanley in 1838, the year before it foundered in Bass Strait. Through a litter of boating equipment, concrete mixer and sheds on the treeless foreshore we follow a brown-black dirt track across the point to the ranger's office and house. This is a courtesy call; officially we should have permits to enter this Aboriginal reserve. The ranger, Frank Woel, is out on patrol so we leave word with his wife to come aboard for drinks later.

He springs aboard at dusk along with three German photographic technicians. Under an American peaked cap he is an extremely bronzed Aryan, lean and fit, his very

The Windfall's awning at Knocker Bay

short shorts strapped with a wide leather belt which holds a hunting knife. A keen photographer of professional standard, Frank has put his knowledge of native flora and fauna and his long experience as a ranger in many corners of the Territory to good and useful purpose. His has been a gradual move away from civilization, driven this last time north from Cannon Hill by uranium mining and Aborigines in cars. He is now reviewing his 'last stand' because V.I.P's. are finding Black Point. Recently he played host to the Governor-General and his entourage. Special accommodation had been built but Lady Cowan asked for a tent because she had never experienced sleeping under canvas. And now the Chief Minister had taken to fishing weekends there.

Whipped by the gusty wind the awning cracks and rolls like thunder. Steel rigging clanks against the aluminium masts and sleep comes only to the exhausted. An oppressive dawn subdues all till the anchor is weighed and the movement of the Windfall under power generates a passage of air.

Little growth remains on the low foreshores of the straits of Port Essington for further cyclones to flatten; slivers of faded yellow and orange sand separate the battered trees and scrub and the grey-green sea.

Big black-violet clouds thunder an appropriate cannonade as the anchor is dropped at noon off the shore of Victoria. Perched on an orange and white clay bluff, just to the east of a sandy beach, is what remains of the sweat and aspirations of mid-last century's settlers: stone chimney stacks in a row like ghostly sentinels, once the hearths of the married quarters, a terrace of tiny Cornish cottages; less remains of the flimsily constructed single quarters. Of the hospital only the foundations and two ovens of its kitchen stand, but the armoury was built to withstand all weather and onslaught, and it has. Projected from the beach below, a solidly constructed jetty of local rocks has weathered many cyclones.

The Hospital Kitchen and Bakery, Victoria, Port Essington.

The Armoury, Victoria, Port Essington.

Nine years after the first northern colonies had been forsaken and just fifty years after the British flag had been raised over Sydney Cove a flotilla of Her Majesty's Ships, Alligator, Britomart and Orontes, commanded by Captain (now Sir Gordon) Bremer, left Sydney loaded with the equipment to establish yet another settlement — prefabricated buildings, stores and domestic animals. Greyhounds, fast enough to bring down kangaroos, had free run of the decks but the cattle, swine, sheep and chooks were confined between the ships' cannons. Below decks the ships were packed tight with Royal Marines, settlers and their families, a full complement of three hundred souls including crews. In retrospect the sailors, who had crewed the vessels from Plymouth to Sydney, no doubt thought that far longer voyage a relatively pleasant cruise.

Losing contact with the Britomart in adverse winds and currents early in the voyage the Alligator and the Orontes made slow progress north till reaching the protection of the Great Barrier Reef and fine sailing conditions.

Increased fear of French, Dutch and even American territorial ambitions had forced Britain's decision to take physical possession once again of Australia's north. Just south of Cape York the ships' companies were put ashore to stretch their legs and witness a formal ceremony of Captain Bremer taking possession of all adjacent land and islands in the name of Her Majesty, Queen Victoria. The Marines fired a volley and all gave three rousing cheers as a large Union Jack unfurled.

At daybreak of the 26th October 1838, nearly six weeks from Sydney, the two ships turned south round Croker Island to

VICTORIA, PORT ESSINGTON

enter the vast outer harbour of Port Essington. A party of Aborigines occupied Record Point and others were seen on the deck of the schooner Essington, anchored offshore. With the help of these friendly Aborigines the frame of a church, which had been prefabricated in Sydney, had already been taken ashore though the site for settlement had yet to be determined.

Ten days later the Britomart arrived to reload the church and deliver it to the western shore of the inner harbour where a table land on a twenty metre high bluff was fired of its tall grass, and stores and buildings were being unloaded. But the church was ill-fated. Within twelve months, before completion, it was violated and levelled by a hurricane. Only the base to its steeple survived the blast to be boarded up and used as a storehouse.

In the same disaster Government House suffered the indignity of being wrenched from its stone piers and dumped three metres away while newly erected cottages were completely demolished. Many boats were destroyed and the H.M.S. Pelorus was driven ashore at Minto Head, the hull submerged in three metres of mud with only its keel visible.

Equally astonished by the destructive power of the wind the Aborigines sought protection and shelter from the settlers. In their store of traditional knowledge there was nothing to describe it — no name for it.

In the early days of the settlement guards had been posted each night but the Aborigines remained friendly. An intensely curious people they would covet certain European articles for which they offered to trade fish, oysters and crabs. Accustomed to roaming naked they began to adorn themselves with articles of clothing, purely as decoration.

All food at Victoria was now rationed. Fruit and vegetable gardens had been devastated in the holocaust, fresh water wells polluted and perishables in the food stores lost. Repairs to the damaged buildings were delayed by monsoonal rains and demands for much higher wages than in Sydney had limited the number of carpenters in the garrison. Simple economics had innovated the prefabrication of buildings but had not made provision for disasters.

But with the rain the gardens were soon fertile. Small plots of pumpkins, cabbages, pineapples, guavas, oranges, lemons, bananas and tamarinds, a legacy from the Buginese, were beginning to fruit. Sadly, much of the fruit fell before it ripened and rats ate the pumpkins. Produce from these private gardens proved inadequate to stem an outbreak of scurvy and the Commandant was not happy about the priorities botanist John Armstrong placed on planting in the public gardens. Armstrong preferred to plant exotics from Rio de Janiero rather than mundane necessities. He claimed that Bremer treated him like a common gardener, ignoring his commission to collect specimens and seeds of native plants for the Royal Botanic Gardens at Kew.

The remoteness of the outpost made it unrealistic to rely upon supply from Sydney. Much closer in climate as well as distance Timor and Indonesia were the obvious sources for the fundamental needs of the colony. Within a month of Victoria's foundation the schooner Essington returned from Kisar, an island controlled by the Dutch, 300 miles to the west, with nineteen buffaloes, sixty pigs, one hundred sheep, poultry, coconuts, banana suckers and various seeds suited to the climate. Rather than coins changing hands goods such as iron and small tools were bartered for tortoise shell, bees-wax and sandalwood. The nearest European settlement was Dilli in Portuguese Timor where the people were friendly and eager to trade. Prices were set for various commodities such as a handkerchief for two hens or a pig was valued at four metres of calico.

Macassan Prau

Praus from Macassar began to put in to Port Essington and permission was granted the Buginese to fish in the area. The Royal Marines found their way of spearing and curing trepang highly diverting. Seventy five Bugis from three praus set up fireplaces and covered the sapling frames of drying sheds or smoke houses with matting. They boiled the trepang in cauldrons, cut them down the centre and boiled them again in salt water with slivers of bark from the mangroves. Finally the trepang was laid on open shelves and smoked in the roughly five by two metres drying sheds on the beach.

Though tolerant of the British local Aborigines were less happy about the presence of the Macassans and violence between them had to be broken up by a strong guard of Marines. Shortly before this incident four Bugis had been killed and seven Aborigines were massacred in retaliation on Goulburn Island. The Macassans had been working this coast for a couple of centuries. In the past they had posted guards of half their numbers to protect those actually fishing. Now, working close to Victoria, fishing was doubly profitable because the settlement's Marines afforded them protection. But their annual visits brought little profit to Port Essington. The Bugis brought fewer and fewer articles to trade because the Dutch authorities imposed such prohibitive duties on British goods taken back to Macassar.

An increasing number of trading vessels visited Victoria and supplies arrived from Sydney but not the promised timber needed for repairs to the damaged buildings. Shortage of building materials was a source of friction between the acting commandant and the commander of the sloop Pelorus, who accused Captain John McArthur of removing some cedar logs from his custody. McArthur, as acting commandant, claimed the timber to re-build the church and threatened to match the force of his Marines against Chambers' naval personnel should there be an attempt to take them back. Tension mounted over a number of such petty issues; the actual command of the garrison was questioned by Chambers and the two officers, refusing to speak directly, though neighbours, resorted to correspondence. On other occasions McArthur had reprimanded Chambers for his corporal punishment of Aborigines before their guilt of petty offences had been established. McArthur had worked hard to maintain good relations between blacks and whites; the goodwill had spread and parties of Aborigines from far inland had visited the settlement. Local blacks had helped with the construction of the buildings and some, having sailed with the Macassans, soon adapted to work on European ships making voyages to Indonesian islands and to Sydney. Racial tolerance was put to a test when a Sergeant of Marines shot and killed an Aborigine attempting escape after arrest with two others for theft.

In reprisal the Aborigines killed not a white but a black, a man called Neinmil, known 'for his good temper and obliging disposition', simply because he was a favourite of the whites.

The garrison had no fear of the Aborigines. In fact the ugly blockhouse with mounted cannons and rusting grapeshot had its back turned on them to face possible aggression by whites from the sea.

Cassowary? after a bark painting from Port Essington, One of the earliest to be collected. →

But it was from the inland that a band of whites approached Victoria. In the heat of the afternoon of December 17th, 1845 five exhausted Europeans, mounted on emaciated horses, and three Aborigines plodded up the hill from Wangi Wangi Cove led by a black known to the garrison as Bill White. Four of the weather-blackened whites were young. The fifth, a quixotic figure, bearded and sparse, presented himself to the Commandant as Dr. Ludwig Leichhardt. It was known that his scientific and exploratory expedition had left Sydney for Port Essington on August 13th of the previous year but hope for survivors had been given up long since. Apart from the harsh terrain and short supplies they had endured attacks by hostile blacks who had speared and killed John Gilbert, the young naturalist of the settlement's earlier days, and wounded others of the party. Of the initial sixteen bullocks all but one had been killed and eaten. Some of this salted meat had disgusted a group of Aborigines encountered while crossing the East Alligator River. Leichhardt recorded their reaction to his lack of civilised amenities: 'You no bread, no flour, no rice, no backie – you no good!' The expedition's spirits had been lifted by friendly blacks at Raffles Bay who offered to guide them to Port Essington. Though close to the end of their physical endurance the exciting prospect of the journey's end just a few hours away kept them awake most of that night. Darling Downs, the last outstation of civilization they had known, was 5000 kilometres and fourteen months behind them.

During the few weeks of convalescence before returning to Sydney on the merchant vessel 'Heroine,' Leichhardt had time to review his life and express views on politics. Quite unimpressed, Captain McArthur, while recognising his talents, deplored Leichhardt's politics referring to him as a thin skinned radical, bitter, virulent, malicious, dishonest, shifty and mean. Nevertheless Ludwig Leichhardt gave his telescope to the Commandant's son with the wish that he remember the visit.

Nelson, the chief mate's Newfoundland dog, rescued survivors of the Heroine when it foundered in Endeavour Strait on its return voyage to Port Essington. From their desparate refuge clinging to the topmasthead of the vessel, which had sunk in six minutes, the captain's Timorese wife with two other Malays and a Roman Catholic missionary, Angelo Confalonieri, were carried to the safety of the reef, one at a time, by that extraordinary dog. Captain McKenzie, master of the vessel, was less fortunate. With his infant daughter strapped to his back he swam away from the wreck till nearing exhaustion some hours later he discovered the child had been dead for quite a time. In the sixth hour he was rescued.

Though not a British subject Father Confalonieri was given shelter and supplies by Captain McArthur. His sacred vessels and vestments had been lost in the wreck but these would have proved useless in his efforts to evangelise the Aborigines. They had neither a particular idolatry nor a concept of religion which might have been replaced by the crucifix and Christian belief. Their nomadic lifestyle precluded teaching; they did not stay long enough in one place to absorb any gospel. But he won their regard as he adopted their nomadic ways in passing from camp to camp sharing his provisions with them and refereeing disputes between clans. An exceptional linguist he was soon able to communicate directly with them and compile vocabularies of the separate languages of seven clans of Aborigines on the Peninsula. However the fun-loving blacks taught him many obscenities which, to their delight, he innocently repeated in his sermons. Angelo Confalonieri complained that Aborigines had 'no understanding but for their belly' and despaired of converting adults though he felt the children could be taught if separated from their parents. Among the blacks there was strong resistance to interference with traditional family life. The frustrated young missionary died of malaria in the hospital at Victoria in 1848.

The following year the third failure to settle the North was admitted and Victoria was abandoned. Fortifications already weakened by termites were blown up and the leaking thatched roofs of hospital and houses were fired. Gifts of unusable tobacco, horses and kangaroo dogs were made to the Aborigines. From the deserted town down to the jetty the Royal Marines marched to the navy band of H.M.S. Meander. A farewell salute of twenty-one guns was fired as the garrison embarked. Forty souls remained in the graveyard. Timor ponies, Banteng cattle and buffaloes were left to roam and become ferine.

In the pea-green pallor of dawn a thick coating of grease over last nights lamb stew is a discouraging start to the day. As he had poured half a box of claret into the pot of fatty chops and vegetables chef Colin had assured me it was a mistake to skim the grease as it was beneficial to health and not at all fattening. To press home this culinary information he is boiling it up again for breakfast. Before anyone touches it Lou is tying down the stove and asking that the pot be placed on deck; Colin obediently puts it down on the weathered carpet in the cockpit but Lou moves it to the deck proper and to Colin's raised eyebrows explains, "I dont want any grease on the Persian rug — it's going to roll out there."

And roll it does as we sail before a strong wind which pushes huge black clouds even faster. It's difficult to draw in the rain on a rolling boat.

From the uncomfortably cold wind and rough sea we find shelter in Knocker Bay. Off a sandy white beach the anchor is dropped not far from a timber jetty that is slowly tumbling into the sea. Nearby two iron-roofed sheds, one stilting out of the water, are rusting to eventual oblivion. Through a chink in the deep violet clouds a ray of sun lights the buildings in a stagy way.

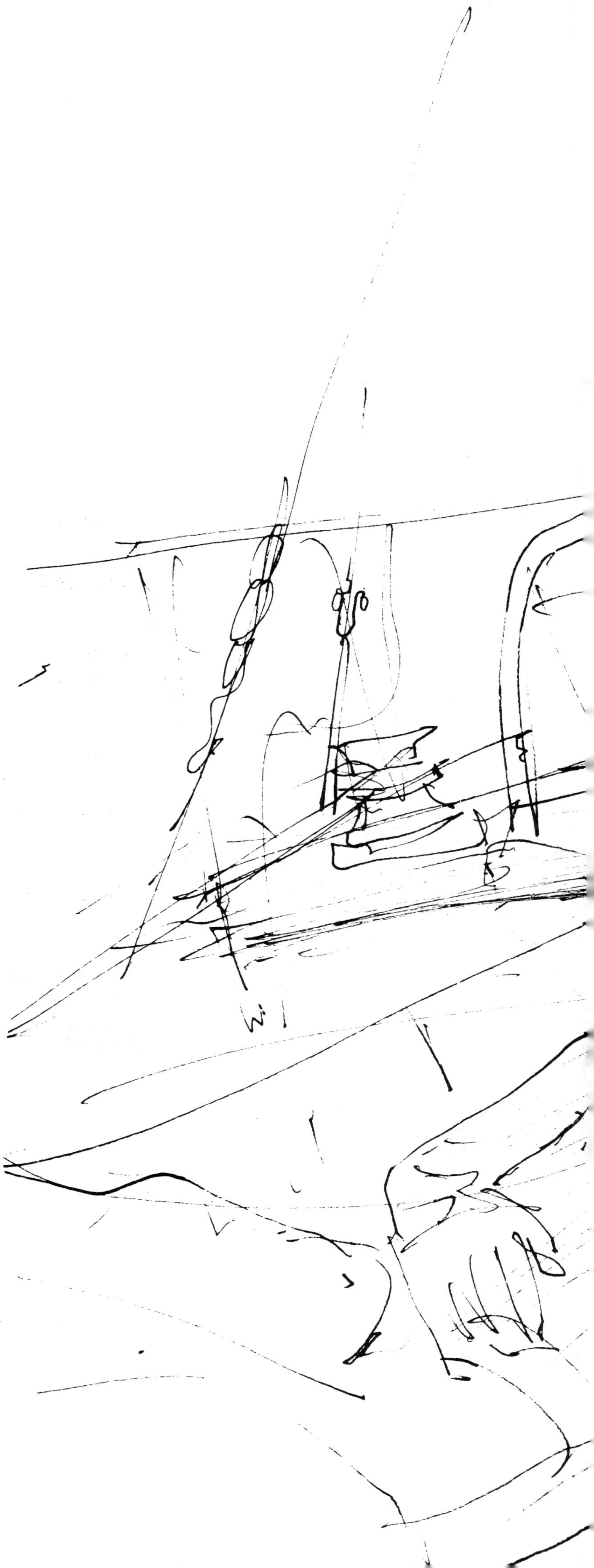

Off Spear Point
4 . 10 . 81

Though windy the cool deck is preferable to the claustrophobic heat of the cabin below. Throughout the night sleep is broken as bed sheets are whipped off by abrupt gusts from the north-west. A flash of red in a cool grey dawn signals more rain so I plan an early start to dinghy ashore and sketch the forsaken pearling settlement which had been built by the Paspaley family not so many years ago.

Pearling Jetty
Knocker Bay

Pearl phallocrypt
from the
Kimberley
◀ region

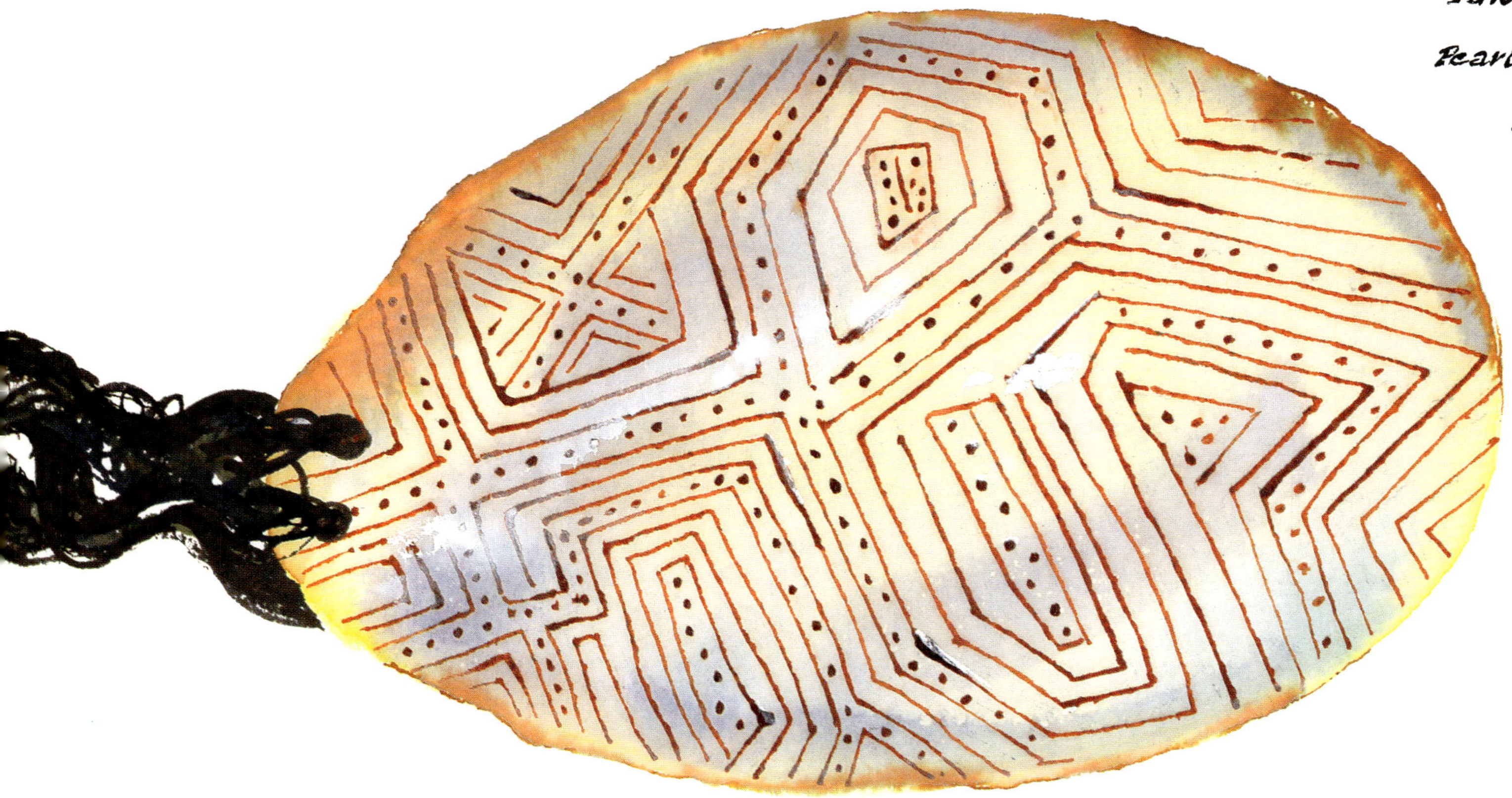

For thousands of years before intruders began to collect pearl-shell for profit along the north coast Aborigines had traded it deep in the interior among people who had no concept of an ocean. If trade over vast distances can be said to be the basis of a viable economy then Aborigines must be considered early in the history of materialism. Artefacts made of pearl-shell from the tropical northern coast have been found near the cold waters of the Southern Ocean thousands of kilometres away. In the extreme north-west shells the size of a small dinner plate were incised with a form of the interlocking key pattern found in Grecian ceramic art. Worn as pendants or penis guards by magic men, or by novices after circumcision ritual then traded for use in rain-making ceremonies.

Abandoned pearling shed – Knocker Bay.

From the sagging jetty a corded timber track leads through the mangroves to a cluster of deserted dwellings in a sordid state of decay. The sheds on the waterfront are partly gutted by fire. Masses of chains and machinery are welded together by rust and coated with salt along with broken baskets and coils of rotten rope. Stacked in cases the large pearl-shells alone remain unaffected by time, but plastic buttons and other synthetic articles have rendered this lustrous shell useless commercially.

Pearling came to the Territory later than the North-west and Torres Strait where multi-racial divers had operated since the 1860s and 1870s. In 1898 three hundred Japanese were based in Darwin. They imported Nagasaki prostitutes at 1890's prices of fifty pounds each. The last Japanese brothel in Darwin was closed in the 1920s.

European divers found severe competition with the cheap Asian labour as prices of pearl-shell dropped, though some managed to make more than a simple living. Xavier Herbert joined a pearling lugger as third diver, sharing the haul, to make enough cash in 1928 to finish a novel and spend a year in Europe; though his lack of diving experience cost him temporary loss of hearing.

Twenty years later there were still sufficient pickings of pearl and shell to support such expert divers as Skipper Dick Saunders and his mate Andy Anderson. Andy needed no plans or books of reference when he restored a superb pearl lugger and a Vietnamese fishing trawler for the Museum of Arts and Sciences in Darwin recently. He recalls that he began diving in 1950 simply for the adventure. In three monthly stints of scouring the sea-bed he was given tucker and sixty pounds (Aust). Asked how he felt the first time the face plate of of his unwieldy diving helmet was bolted tight he replied, "Bloody scared", but could find no words for the exhilaration he found on breaking the surface after dives of twenty and more fathoms. And of a cyclone he recalled the solid sea whipped to spray with the force of powerful punches to the face so painful he covered it with a towel as he steered away from the eye of the storm. His own eyes were temporarily sightless and skin had been torn from his face. Yet he regrets having missed cyclone Tracy. He was in Singapore sitting down to Yum Cha the Christmas day Darwin was blown off the map. In a flash-back to the early 1950s he spoke of the 'Rear-Admiral' who had lived in the broken stern of a hulk on Francis Beach. This eccentric recluse was the painter Ian Fairweather who was to astonish the crew of a pearling lugger far out in the Timor Sea when he

looked up from his flimsy little raft and asked politely of the black skipper, "Excuse me Sir, am I on the right course for Timor?" Though assured he was on course the triangular three metre raft constructed of three wartime aircraft belly tanks laced together with fencing wire and old rope, so unstable it toppled when he stood, was swept past the mainland of Timor. On the sixteenth night Fairweather, who had been accompanied by two sea-birds and escorted by sharks for most of the voyage, was washed over a reef at Roti, the last speck of an island off the west coast of Indonesian Timor. The sixty-years-old Scot collapsed on the beach. His remarkable feat was rewarded with two months in gaol and deportation. Of the raft much remains on Roti: the 'decking' planks have been built into a dwelling and at least one of the belly tanks, halved, serves as wash tub and basin.

Ten years after the 1956–57 peak in the pearl-shell industry the bottom dropped out of the market; the sole legacy has been a virile strain of Malay, Asian, Indonesian and Filipino blood. Culture-pearl farming such as the venture at Knocker Bay replaced shell gathering. The Paspaleys temporarily abandoned this settlement to concentrate on farming beds elsewhere. (They have since returned.)

A large pleasure schooner with a windowed galleon stern drops anchor beyond the tumbling jetty to the leeward of the 'Windfall'. Concentration on a sketch of the desolate pearling shed is disturbed as a dinghy is beached and the Rhodesian skipper of the schooner, the 'Alegrias', warns me a hunting party will be shooting Banteng cattle in this vicinity after breakfast. I ask what pleasure will they derive from shooting docile domestic cattle; those I have encountered have stood in dumb curiosity. However this skipper with cap and George V greybeard who sails his boat to expensive charter assures me that these beasts are wild and ferocious in charges which forced the hunter to shoot. Banteng are much smaller than buffalo; displayed on a trophy room wall their horns would be a joke. Their flesh has a sweet and delicate flavour but the hunters leave the carcass where it falls. They pay $2000 for a permit to indulge in this macho sport and there is talk of Aboriginal Traditional Owners demanding a further $200 for each animal shot. Let's hope they, at least, enjoy the meat.

On board the 'Windfall' I report the planned shooting to Lou who has doubts about wealthy playboys' ability to hit the right target. As the first shots are fired we weigh anchor and sail for Oyster Point to indulge in the more meaningful task of food gathering. On the point under a red bluff the oysters are large and soon we are well supplied for lunch.

How to fly Colin back for conference with the Chief Minister preoccupies the afternoon's sailing. Brisbane is crystal clear but much nearer Darwin is blocked out. The 'Alegrias' has a more powerful transmitter but her decks are deserted as we sail by. Sheltering inside the entrance to Port Essington a trawler drapes its nets against a murky sky like a cormorant drying its wings. Coming alongside the N.S. 'Anson' a line is tossed and secured. Among the faces looking down on us are a couple familiar from the Darwin Sailing Club, Alan the skipper and the 'Anson's cook Marlene. By the 'Windfall's' bowsprit we board the stern of the larger vessel where the crew toss us tins of cold beer, our first in forty-eight hours due to a sad miscalculation by our victualler. Alan suggests we relax over another beer and join him on a trawl. Lou cast off and dropped anchor happy to have his boat

to himself, get some housework done and have a kip. Housework on the 'Anson' is long overdue; every line, rail and member of the crew is black with grease but everything runs smoothly and is free of rust. Way up on the bridge behind the complex controls is a car-seat strapped and fixed in a tub. From the comfort of this vantage point the power that lifts the trawler to plane and bounce over the choppy sea is exhilarating — unreal; just minutes ago we had been under sail, the real thing, at a stately five or six knots. The lacy steel nets screen the sun demurely like gigantic mantillas before they smack the surface hard and rape the sea-bed of its shellfish. Power is cut and the vessel wallows as the nets break the surface and swing inwards to spill the haul on to the hatch. The rejects, stunned and damaged by the massive hit, are returned to the deep and the selected healthy specimens are committed to the deep-freeze. Such deadly efficient trawling has seriously disturbed the breeding habits of crustaceans on the sea-bed. An increasing scarcity of shellfish in northern coastal waters has caused the authorities to restrict the number of licensed trawlers.

Oil slicks on the deck reflect the wind-blown flames of a barbecue as Alan tosses a platter of cooked blue swimmer crabs, huge tiger-prawns and Moreton Bay bugs overboard. "Too cold," he says, "plenty more where they came from." Sharks, blue whalers, tigers, hammerheads, a metre to three and four in length circling the trawler are clear in the deeply penetrating lights. These shine constantly, powered by batteries needed for refrigeration. The engines which generate the charge never stop so trawlers are forever festive, lit up like Christmas trees.

In Wellington boots and padded gloves at midnight I descend into the frozen wilderness of refrigeration in a kind of trawlers initiation. Curiosity is soon satisfied but my return to the tropics is slowed down by a heavy foot on my head. My body feels like an Alaska bomb as it thaws later in the engine room, an exclusively yellow world of throbbing power, batteries and tangled wires

Replete with beer and prawns walking the rolling 'Windfall's' bowsprit is hazardous. With eyes adjusting to the dark, toes are stubbed and a shoulder sprained. Colin's cap, pipe and pouch are retrieved from the sea and we turn in below leaving him in the cockpit munching cheese and biscuits with a glass of red. Shortly after dawn, checking out his boat, Lou complains that the cockpit is littered with crumbs, tobacco and ash. From the sea a voice asks politely. "Excuse me. Hello" Over the bow Lou looks down on a floating beard which presents Colin's face as though on a platter. Hanging on to the anchor chain he explains, "Sorry old chap, can't think how I got here — been floating around the trawler, blinded by the lights. Thought I was in Botany Bay. Seems I've been swimming for hours." Lou ties a noose and throws the rope down saying, "Slip this around your neck and I'll pull you out." As he warms up his famous stew for breakfast he adds curry powder and washes the mess down with a glass of the boxed red. With a bucket of sea-water he swills himself down to face the day.

Burrunguy (Nourlangie rock)
—Black and white hunters of the feral buffalo shared a unique lifestyle in the shooters' camps.
—Aboriginal artists discuss the rock art of their ancestors at Burrunguy, a spiritual gathering shelter, a place for ritual and dance.
—The Alligator rivers floodplain, haven to animal and bird life, is a gigantic supermarket for Aborigines

Though Banteng cows on the Cobourg Peninsula drop a disproportionate number of stillborn calves a thousand and more of these feral cattle roam in herds larger than in their original Timor breeding grounds. Too timid to run the blockade of crocodile infested swamps these small beasts are confined on the peninsula.

But the huge water buffaloes soon crashed a passage through the mangroves to penetrate inland. Revelling in the mud and humid heat they became the first settlers to thrive in Arnhem Land. Some of the first of the expanding herds were encountered near Oenpelli by the first white men to cross the Kakadu, Leichhardt's expedition of 1845.

In the wet these domesticated cattle took up home ranges with areas for camping, feeding and drinking, for wallowing and rubbing against trees. As the waters receded from the floodplains in the intensifying dry season these ferine animals converged on the billabongs of the Kakadu which for thousands of years had been the rich source of food and ceremony for many Aboriginal clans. Wading from water hole to billabong buffalo herds channelled the freshwater to tidal rivers and the coast. Billabongs which had held fresh water through past dry seasons began to backfill with salt water and king tides flooded in to change areas of fertile freshwater swamp into arid, saline clay. River banks were broken by their

wallowing to expose the roots of trees which were swept away in the next wet. With flagrant disregard for their adopted country these enormous herbivores often relieved themselves while bathing. The chemicals produced by such abandoned behaviour create a scum on still fresh water such as can be seen on billabongs at Nourlangie and Jim Jim. Evidence of this impact on the ecology was recorded by Leichhardt: after crossing the East Alligator River he "encamped at a good sized waterhole at the bed of this creek, the water of which was covered with a green scum .... the dung and tracks of buffaloes were fresh."

The healthy economy of coastal communities had its roots in the diversity of its food sources (more recently Aborigines have referred to Arnhem Land as a 'supermarket'). The introduced buffalo was welcomed as a plentiful supply of red meat but the price was high — the loss of other food sources and finally the quality of life. Dave Lindner made this clear six years ago but much earlier warnings had been ignored. In a resource evaluation of Government land between the East and South Alligator Rivers in 1886 Captain Carrington reported: " .... large herds of buffalo numbering several hundreds were seen daily.... these animals are increasing rapidly and if some preventative measures are not taken it is only a question of time when they will increase so as to become a serious evil."

Prior to this, in the early 1870s white men began to realise a potential in buffalo beef and hide. John Lewis was the first to take up pastoral leases in Arnhem Land. On his way to establish the Cobourg Cattle Company in 1875 his party was attacked by hostile Aborigines. Disadvantaged on foot Lewis and his men had been cutting reeds to corduroy a crossing of the East Alligator River. From the camouflage of three metres tall grass, hardwood-tipped reed spears were thrown from womeras and shots were fired in defending repeated attacks. At the end of his journey a relieved Lewis was greeted by the friendly Aborigines of Port Essington who said they already knew of the hostile encounters — an efficient bush telegraph existed then. The white men built a bark hut at foresaken Victoria and laid a floor of bricks salvaged from ruins. Aborigines supplied these new settlers with geese, fish, turtles and eggs, oysters, yams and wild honey, a diversity of food enhanced by the Chinese cook. Lewis noted that the Aborigines made dugout canoes yet hated the Macassans who had shown them the craft.

Buffalo which had been abandoned to the wild were again corralled, Timor ponies were broken-in for riding and the Banteng provided succulent red meat. Within a year or two Lewis had left the peninsula but E.O. Robinson, an 'English gentleman recluse,' stayed a further thirty years. With Aboriginal help he built up stocks of cured hides for trade with the Macassans and became the first to capitalise on the buffalo.

On the wetlands of the Kakadu buffalo had bred in alarming numbers. Paddy Cahill, an early pioneer of the buffalo industry, said he had seen a mob of six hundred on the Alligator Rivers' plains. He shot sixteen hundred in the dry season of 1897. Along with unique characters of the 1880s and 1890s, such as 'Buffalo Joe' Cooper the virtual king of Melville Island, Cahill's horsemanship and shooting became legend. Galloping with a stampeding herd and aiming to paralyse with a bullet to the spine demanded cool nerve. Accuracy was crucial because a wounded bull could be dangerous. Their horns spreading to two and a half metres have ripped horses from under shooters, many of whom were gored, particularly the skinners, Aborigines on foot. Such incidents earned this normally docile animal the reputation of an aggressive, savage beast.

On a typical 'run' mounted shooters would gather in the already oppressive heat of dawn under a cover of mosquito infested paperbarks. Staring dumbly at first a mob of perhaps a hundred buffaloes would soon wheel and stampede as the riders broke out on to the boggy plain. As the horse brought a shooter alongside a selected target the buffalo would weave and the horse, bred and trained for this kind of play, would manoeuvre with it, sure-footed and wise to the potential of bull's horns — spread much wider than those of the brave bulls of Portugal and sometimes Spain, which are fought from horseback. As the wild eyed buffalo and horse galloped neck and neck the shooter would stand in the stirrups, swing a leg over to crouch low and drop the barrel of his Winchester to almost touch the buffalo's spine. At point blank range there was no error; the beast fell and the horse swung away sharply as the rider vaulted back into the saddle selecting another cartridge from his bandolier — the ejected shell span in the dust while the horse overtook the next victim. Paddy Cahill recorded a tally of forty-six in one 'run'. Like shearers, shooters took pride in their tallies.

The crippled buffaloes, may be sixty or more, lay on the open plain for hours, sometimes days, at the skinners' mercy, the coup de grâce. The skin of a dead animal soon decays in humid tropical heat. Kept alive, though immobilised by the spinal shot, the hide remains warm and supple, easy to remove. The hides were thrown over packhorses and carried to the main camp for salting and drying by Aborigines. Each year a lugger would put into a remote landing in the mangroves to take aboard another thousand or two hides.

Base camps were set up near water, not so much for the game it attracted as to facilitate the washing of hides. The early camps were on the steep banks of rivers, a protection against crocodiles, where boats could bring in supplies and hides could be shipped out. As more and more hunters shot-out the flood plains the buffaloes resorted to higher land in the valleys of the escarpment. These less boggy areas advantaged the shooters to work earlier in the season. To service the extended activity over greater distances staging camps were organised.

Enclosed by residual rocks a deep, clear waterhole with white sand beach shaded by paperbarks and twisting pandanus at Little Nourlangie was an oasis for staging shooters and skinners. The tranquillity of this camp was disturbed only by saltwater crocodiles which had transgressed by way of the tidal rivers in flood and adapted to the sweet fresh water. For thousands of years this had been a traditional site. Since childhood the Aboriginal members of the shooting parties had speared barramundi in the waterhole and wallaby on the rocks which provided shelter during the wet. They called it Nawulandja. Nourlandjie, the European spelling, is close phonetically.

Buffalo beef and the life style in camp were shared and white man's rations of flour for damper, treacle, jam and tea complimented the more substantial bush tucker of fish, wildfowl, walleroo, water lily bulbs and yams. At the end of the shooting season the blacks were given wet season rations of sugar, flour and tobacco which, in the grand manner of itinerates in the outback, they blew in a get-together before reverting to their traditional hunter-gatherer existence, spending time at important ceremonial sites to perform appropriate ritual. They used this time to return the bones of those who had died while working away from their homelands. Alongside and often superimposed on earlier traditional paintings they began to record images of introduced animals and the activities of Europeans, ships and guns.

◀Contact art.▶

'Blue painting'▶ The blue pigment is Reckitts washing blue, a new and exciting colour for Aboriginal artists.

Most Aboriginal men had at times painted on the rock faces of their shelters. They displayed no respect for the work of others and painted over 'old masters' of perhaps 20,000 years earlier. Expression was of primal importance — art as such did not exist for them. Unintentionally they produced works of art and the superimposition of painting upon painting built an intriguing dimensional depth like centuries of graffiti on an ancient city wall. Occasionally the work of a talented artist survived undisfigured as do the paintings of Najombolmi of the Badmardi, a clan who till recent years visited the shelters of Anbangbang and Nangaluwurr at Nourlangie Rock. As a buffalo shooter, gold miner and stockman he was known to Europeans as Barramundi Charlie. Through life long experience over vast areas he had become aware of increasing change in the ways of his people. Disillusionment through contact with Europeans had led to loss of ritual knowledge and rendered their art meaningless. The year before his death, in 1964 he returned to the Anbangbang shelter and in a conscious effort to revive or at least commemorate the beliefs and art of the people who had once lived there he created a large painting on rock face in Xray style. By symbolising milk in the breasts of some women in the two family groups Najombolmi attempted to breathe life back into the shelter. Good and evil, in this last important rock painting, are depicted in the images of Namarrgon the Lightning man and Namandjolg, a fearsome spirit.

In the wet season of the shooters' camp years when painting was still involved in ritual the hunter-gatherers sheltering here would venture across the floodplains on rafts among the nests of magpie geese collecting just a few eggs from each.

Magpie geese
also called Pied geese.

The billabong is vast after the wet. Great flocks of water fowl are an uplifting sight. A chorus of honks and grunts comes from a wide variety of species — pied herons stilting in ranks, tiny brown waders in the shallows flicking their tails saucily from side to side as they fossick for insects, strings of ibis, pygmy duck, teal, shelduck, black duck, whistling duck, spoonbill, pelican, jabiru but the most abundant are the magpie geese. The swampy region around Nourlangie is the only place in the world where such numbers congregate. They dont appear to be as well put together as other species of geese. Their unusually long legs (yellow) support a heavy body and a conical hump on the head looks like a party cap. But the white cummerbund encircling the black body is dashing. As one bird swims closer it is possible to identify the brown of its eye set

in the flesh red of its bare face and upper bill. Difficult to tell the sex of a magpie goose but the female is slightly shorter than the male (80cms to 90cms). Both sexes honk resonantly, the male's pitched higher is immediately answered by the female.

Early in the wet geese begin to pair off. Many males mate with two females and the trio will share a nest. First stage in nesting is the construction of a platform to float it. The male does most of the building by bending and trampling spike rush, their favoured food. As the platform is used for both courting and resting the birds are constantly weaving in more clumps of rush to make it more substantial. Finally when eggs are laid the nest is formed as a thickly woven deep cup. All birds, male and female, share incubation duties. In the heat of day a goose will stand to shade the eggs rather than sit. Each female lays six to nine eggs so a ménage à trois could produce a large family indeed.

As the floodwaters receded on the wetland plains magpie geese, which gaggled in the diminishing billabongs, were speared or, from a hide of reeds, knocked down with a stick as they flew low overhead. Turtle too were speared or taken by hand. Though expert fishermen themselves even a novice like myself found turtles easy prey to a lure. The rivers of southern New Guinea were the only known habitat of the Fly River turtle till less than twenty years ago when it was identified from a painting on a rockface near Nawulandja or Little Nourlangie water-hole.

Carettochelys insculpta

after one of the "blue paintings" in a rock shelter near Nawalandja waterhole

For centuries the Fly River turtle has been preferred tucker amongst Aborigines. But it was not till 1969 that Europeans, through images in rock paintings, recognised its existence in rivers of the N.T. Aptly named the pig-nose this soft-shelled turtle is Australia's only freshwater example. When challenged its fore-flippers quickly flick mud or sand over its carapace in its only defence, camouflage.

The long-necked tortoise.
Chelodina rugosa.

Sensing danger the long-necked tortoise uses a similar ploy, burying itself up to its alert eyes. To lure a fish in closer this chelid retracts its neck then fully extends it to strike and suck in the prey.

On a line set earlier in the day we pulled a long-necked tortoise from the river. To share among the six of us boiling seemed the reasonable way of cooking it — at least each of us would taste the soup. But there was plenty for anyone who could masticate the rubbery flesh and the soup was the foulest of turtle — perhaps we hadn't cleaned it thoroughly. Nipper told us later that turtle is best cooked by first gutting it through a cut near a rear leg, then cleansing in water before placing it legs up on hot coals, grilling slowly to prevent burning the shell. When the legs crack easily serve on the shell.

At the southern end of the Mount Brockman – Nourlangie Rock massif a mammoth lion in stratas of weathered stone rests in a sea of dry grass. In the wet season water spilling from the Arnhem Land plateau, the sculptor of this powerful form, floats and reflects the lion – the mind takes a quick trip to Gibraltar. Scientists say the foundations for Burrunguy, this important feature of the Kakadu, were laid 1600 million years ago. Time has whittled the inside of Burrunguy to expose its conglomerate core. Sheer walls of pink ochre vertically streaked black and white tower over collapsed sandstone which formed shelters to be occupied some 50,000 years ago by Aborigines.

Though Burrunguy is central to the territory of the Warramal of the Gundjeitmi-speaking people distant clans of differing language groups gathered here to participate in ceremonies. Hunting and gathering on one another's territory it was a sharing community. Among clans ritual differed but they shared the belief that all creatures and features in the landscape were created by ancestor beings who instructed spirit beings to populate and teach the traditions which are still celebrated in design, song and dance. Song is poetry which, together with expression through dance, breathes

life into ritual performed in the
around camp fires. Certain songs
particular people while others are
Thus in a non-literate society ideas,
history are transmitted and perpetuated.
and such as were performed to induce
Some are expressive acts of pure
entertainment. Both vocally and
brilliant mimics. Their close association
creatures naturally attunes them to
mime and dance. The brolga is an

flickering shadows of flames
and dances are sacred to a
traded and cross clan boundaries.
tenets of culture and knowledge of
Apart from secret-sacred rituals
rain or to put a jinx on an enemy
mime and dance simply for
in movement Aborigines are
with the landscape and its
be whatever they choose to
enchanting example of this

rump paler grey
wing span 2m
Brolga stands taller than a metre

naked crown
green-grey
green grey
bill
Dewlap
black
primary
wing feathers
darker

Nest is a platform
in swamp. Brolgas
are monogamous.
Incubation is shared
and after a young bird
is hatched the couple
stay together

Throwing back its head in sheer exhuberance the brolga trumpets a grating call, a surprisingly harsh note from such an elegant bird. Of the dancing crane family brolgas are the lightest of foot. Stilting in grassy swamp a bird will toss a twig into the air then bow to his partner who shakes her half-spread wings as the pair bob and strut on their long spindly legs. Soon the flock forms rows facing each other to bow in courtly gesture before advancing and retiring in dance movement of exact measure. As though bored with the formality a bird sometimes leaps into the air to 'chute back to earth on wings of two metres span. This stately dance routine prompted an old fossicker at Jim Jim to tell us, "You know these 'native companions', well they get together on moonlit nights and dance a quadrille."

Long ago Aboriginal clans choreographed a brolga dance which they still perform while telling the story of a beautiful young girl called Buralga, an original dancer of enchanting grace. Most women were content to clap sticks and chant to dancing of the men but Buralga was possessed and danced in her own expressive way. Her fame spread and many men wanted her but she rejected all. One became angry saying if he could not have her nobody would. So one day as Buralga danced he enveloped her in a willi willi. When the magical whirlwind of dust moved on she appeared in the form of a tall silver-grey bird never before seen. Without hesitation the bird danced the steps of Buralga. The people called her name and the bird appeared to respond. Thus the bird was called brolga.

Expression is free in the brolga dance. Running, walking and stalking in a circle the men beat their elbows and stamp the dust. The beating becomes furious as the dancers line up before the musicians, now obscure in a cloud of dust. The star performance is a routine of long and high jumps, kicking up their heels against their buttocks while sweeping

back their arms
in circular movement.
Another dancer stilts
on one leg with the
other extended, poised
like a cautious bird.
The troupe build up
the pace to a climactic
frenzy then stop suddenly,
standing motionless to miss a
beat of the rhythm before
continuing the circular performance.

The dance of the buffalo tells a story in easy-to-follow realistic mime. Interpretations vary among clans but usually the star performer sprouts horns by holding the straight branch of a sapling across the back of his shoulders and, stooping, paws the earth with his feet. Melville Islanders mime the buffalo with arms fully extended as horns in an energetic dance moving shoulders, hips and ribs in vibrant rhythm. Here the 'hunters' in file shuffle to a slower, clapped rhythm. Features in the landscape become stage props, tree to climb to observe and rocks to shelter behind when the buffalo charges. Early in the performance buffalo menaces hunters who flee but when finally speared he falls, then leaps to his feet and joins the chorus in pounding the dust, a high knee action which stops dramatically on the last stick beat.

Some clans rely more on mime and less on voice, apart from a scream of pain or a triumphant yell. Others shout in unison at the end of a rhythmic movement while many shout or repeat a call high in pitch like a bird or low in a growl. Aboriginal music is primarily vocal and like that of south east Asia heavily nasal. Both follow a monotonous melodic line that is certainly not based on instrumental tuning but the nasal production to the resounding open-handed slap on thighs and clack-clack of sticks with an over-drone of didjeridu is haunting.

Secret-sacred dances are usually performed before an exclusively male audience. When produced in mixed company women are obliged to cover their eyes during certain sequences. The stars are exclusively male and spontaneity is the essence of the dance yet at all times perfect timing with the clap-sticks is maintained.

Women sometimes participate in a chorus line of shuffle-hop-kick which looks simple enough but could be as difficult to master as the dance of the cygnets in Swan Lake. They have their own songs of 'love-magic' and dances which exclude men. Such rituals are danced with an abandonment never displayed before men.

Buffalo dance, Melville Is.

Alkajko, an associate of Namargon, the Lightning Man. (detail of female spirit figures in the Nangaluwur shelter near Nourlangie Rock)

The dancing position of this figure was thought by an Aboriginal adviser to be inappropriate — hence the drawing has been masked.

F. H.

Bargini, wife
of Narmargon
the Lightning Man.
(detail from the
rock painting by
Najombolmi at the
AnbangBang Shelter
Nourlangie Rock)

In the midday heat of June 1978 floating among the palmy reflections of Nawulandja's clear water Kate and I felt the serenity of this oasis had not been disturbed since some spirit being had created it. Yet eighty years back this waterhole had been the site of a busy staging camp for buffalo shooters, blacks sharing one of their popular resorts with whites.

Close direct contact had had little impact on the life style of either and none on the ecology — saved it, in fact, by eradicating most of the buffalo. But that, of course, was before beer cans, plastic and 'off-road' vehicles' had been invented.
Two years later we were confronted by a notice board at the water's sandy beach prohibiting swimming and warning of sharks and salt water crocodiles. On visits

over the next five years I noted: beer cans alongside human remains in a burial chamber; within a few months the skull had been looted and replaced with a further scatter of cans; sharks and crocodiles no longer appeared on the notice-board which still prohibits swimming; other notices now declare heavy fines for defacing rock art and entering sacred areas. A rapidly developing tourist industry is imposing the greatest threat to Aboriginal traditional life and to the ecology.

In 1962, two years before Najombolmi painted his major work at Anbangbang, English naturalist David Attenborough recorded the painted walls of this shelter. The first to film the early weathered images he was also the last because they were soon lost under the last attempts to perpetuate the art of rock painting. At that time Attenborough found evidence of Aboriginal occupation of the shelter in bedding of sheets of bark laid on a sapling platform and stone pestles in smoothly ground mortar hollows on a 'table' rock. On the ground were chunks of ochre and stone scrapers. At the back was a burial chamber with a number of skeletons and ceremonial objects. All have gone — souvenired.

Petrophassa rufipennis

Before this few Europeans had disturbed the timid rock wallabies or startled the chestnut-quilled rock pigeons to take off with a resounding clap of wings and to whir in bursts of rapid wing-beats between glides as they made for cover in a fissure or narrow rock ledge, running on very short legs as they touched down.

Later in the 1960s safari operators worked a trail through the rocks and scrub on the northern side of the Mt. Brockman-Nourlangie massif to the large occupational shelter of Nangaluwur, then on to Anbangbang of Burrungiy and from there to Nawulandja. During the wet months this waterhole is swollen by Nourlangie and Bandalg creeks. In the dry as water drained back to the creeks by a narrow channel, which formed a natural fish trap, a pair of sea eagles claimed the territory alongside Aborigines with spears. Nearby Nourlangie billabong was choked with water-lilies and varied species of wading birds sharing the easy pickings.

As far as we can see we are the only audience. So it seems these large raptores are putting on a show of their magnificent flying skills just for us. The osprey plunge-dives to climb again to a great height then repeats this aerobatic stunt.

In contrast the white-breasted sea eagle soars magnificently as though conserving energy for the final act. Flying lower now we can see a fish clutched in the osprey's talons. At slightly higher altitude the eagle slowly beats its powerful wings and begins to harry the smaller bird. In panic the osprey drops its prey leaving the larger bird to swoop to earth and claim the catfish for its own.

The white-breasted sea eagle maintains a territory and is king of it. But we have watched terns and other smaller birds fighting and protecting their nesting sites against this predator.

To me it's cry is a peculiar crackling noise. Others hear it as a kind of clanging 'clank-clank'. But we agree it also calls 'onk-onk' like a goose and much louder. During breeding season they perform sustained duets.

the male is 76cms
female is larger - 84 cms
Wingspan about 2m.

Wings, back and
part of tail black to dark ash-grey
Head, neck and underparts including
tail are white.

Diameter of nest more than 2m.
These are made of sticks and
lined with leaves, placed
in tall trees as high as 30m.
At times it nests on
projecting rock ledges.
Nests have been known
to have been in use
for years in succession.

A/p The Arnhem Experience Frank Hodgkinson '80

Rock Wallaby – Petrogale lateralis

An easy walk from Burrunguy across the plain the water hole of Nawulandja is approached between residual rocks. A crevice in the steep northern side of the ravine is believed by local clans to have been cleft by Badbong, the rock wallaby. In the shade below a sparkling pool provides drinking water during the dry season. The pass opens to parkland accented by dark sandstone studded with shining white quartz.
Digging at this site archeologists have found bones, stone tools, shells and ochre which yielded evidence of occupation for more than 10,000 years. Fresh water mussels found here were proven to be a relatively recent introduction but for all those years Aborigines had speared rock wallabies, water birds, fish, native cats, possums, bandicoots and smaller marsupials.

Spiny-tailed gecko
Diplodactylus ciliaris
length 13 cms.

Velvet gecko
Oedura marmorata
length 15cms →

Hiding behind
spangled bark
or under stones
in banded shade
the gecko's
camouflage is
its only defence.
The evasive patterns
of lizards are
transformed into
dramatic abstractions
by Aboriginal artists.

Twenty metres across the pool where water trickles from a cleft in the rock a handsome monitor dives in and disappears. Within seconds it surfaces almost within reach and with little hesitation eases its sleek wet body on to the warm rock beside me — more than a metre from the tips of its yellow forked tongue to the end of the grey cross hatched tail. As it tucks into my biscuits the scales of its body are cool against my thigh. Too close for detached observation — it had been easier to sketch as it approached.

Back in the water with limbs pressed against the sides of its body the vertically compressed tail propels the monitor in the agile manner of crocodiles. The Merton water monitor fishes mostly underwater. Walking

on the bottom with eyes open it preys on frogs, large water insects, fish and crustaceans. On land this expertly adapted semi-aquatic hunter catches lizards and small mammals.
the female lays as many as nine eggs on leaf mould in a chamber of a carefully constructed burrow. the entrance to which is then sealed

Varanus Mertensi

Yellow-billed Spoonbill
stands about 90 cms
Flapping her wings the female pecks aggressively at her male suitor. They bob heads up and down as the male tries to nibble her bill. The bond is formed when he achieves this.

Its long stride is slow yet the short side to side strokes of its bill are quick to grab fish and insects that may touch the inside of its spoon-shaped tip — with a toss of the head the spoonbill swallows. The mating female makes the initial nesting gesture by tugging on a twig. The male clamps on the same twig as he mounts her. He then collects materials while she constructs the nest. The pair preen one another and clap their bills while sharing incubation of the eggs
Royal Spoonbill
about 75 cms tall. frequently seen in mixed flocks with other species.

Flying out of Mudginbarri we told the pilot of our attempts to see paintings at the base of Mount Brockman, attempts frustrated by sacred ritual for the death of a clan elder. Clipping the tree tops the obliging young man took us directly and climbing steeply seemed to run the wheels up the sheer mountain face. As the 'plane banked I could have reached out and touched the rock — we would never get closer to the home of the Rainbow Serpent, who must have resented the rude awakening. The weathered facade of Brockman shimmering in the afternoon sun reminded me of Rouen Cathedral and Claude Monet's paintings of pure light.

tches of dawn on Mount Brockman (the massif seen from Baroalba spring)

As the major portion of Aboriginal food was gathered from vegetation the digging stick proved more efficient than the spear. Since mostly women collected plant food they could claim to be the fundamental breadwinners. Few men hunt these days but some of the women continue their traditional role. Perhaps high prices in supermarkets at Oenpelli and Jabiru for flour, sugar, fish and a local shortage of fresh fruit and vegetables turn them back to fish and fossick for food in their homelands. They never think of this activity as monotonous drudgery, as a housewife may about domestic chores; it is a daily event, an outing, a chance to gossip and while away leisure hours while gathering good things to eat. Between naps and chatter over a few hours they collect sufficient for immediate need and never hoard hence waste is minimal and plenty is left to gather tomorrow.

In October 1984 driving from Jabiru we stopped before the turn to Oenpelli to pick up a party of Aborigines on foot, four women of various ages, a teenaged girl and three children, carrying dilly bags, plastic bags, bark baskets and digging sticks. One of the little boys proudly clutched a nylon fishing line. They had not thumbed a lift but gladly accepted taking their own good time to climb on to the open tray of the truck. Chatting nasally they told of plans for the day and at their yelled request we dropped them near Ja Ja billabong. On our return journey from Cannon Hill four hours later we paused to watch the children splashing in play and the older women cooking over a fire on the bank. The younger women waded among the water-lilies running a hand down the leaf stalks to locate the root tubers and dig them out. In breast deep water they felt for the elusive rhizome with their toes deep in the soft mud. In sunlit clear deeper water they dived and remained under some time to prise the firmly implanted bulbs from the bottom. Soon they swam and waded ashore to warm themselves by the fire and roast some of the roots. The remainder were piled into bags along with a couple of catfish and some smaller specimens, which the children had caught in their hands, to take home.

And home, where we dropped them off near the turn to Jabiru township, was a cluster of small concrete grey bungalows hidden from the road in a clump of eucalypts and floating in a backwater swamp of discarded cans and plastic.

Recently built under mining lease terms to house families of the traditional owners of this land these domestic buildings already looked like a cyclone had blasted the windows and torn doors from their hinges — damage which had in fact been done by the tenants, doors and windows kicked out to allow the landscape in. In designing these fundamental structures no thought had been given to the Aborigines way of life — they may not be enclosed.

Yet one wonders why they choose to live in this squalor rather than by the billabongs with the green smell of lily pads. Actually, the flowers, splendid in colours and forms, have no scent at all. Every part of the water-lily supplies nourishment; leaf, flower, fruit stalk and root stock provide the most abundant source of food in Arnhem Land. The leaves of the Lotus lily, sometimes a metre across, stand well above the water, at times taller than the flowers. After stripping off the tough outer fibre the lower part of the leaf-stalk looks like and is crisp like celery but has less flavour. In polluted water Aborigines nipped off and pinched the stalks at their base and drank pure water from the hollow tube. Shaped like a broad spinning-top the fruit matures after the petals fall and contains pea-sized nuts in cavities on the upper surface. As the nuts ripen they rattle loose. These were eaten raw, roasted or boiled. Leichhardt wrote of the seeds 'when roasted and pounded, made a most excellent substitute for coffee.' People of South east Asia, where the Lotus is sacred, use this food. Similarly the fruit of the Giant Water-lily was collected before it split and sank to root more plants. The whole fruit was roasted but only to release the seeds which look like caviar. Raw they have the subtle flavour of sunflower seeds; lightly fried they are delicious though crunchy — known to Aborigines as Wuridjonga. The root tubers or Parijiliji baked in hot ashes taste like chestnut. Cakes and dampers were made from baked, pounded and ground seed. Tasting like wholemeal and said to be more nutritious lily-cakes or Munduaii were a special offering by women at mourning ceremonies to older men. Younger men were forbidden to touch them.

A tooth knocked out ceremonially was buried beside a billabong to help the lilies grow. On death a body is placed on a tree platform to be picked clean by birds. The sun-bleached bones were then placed in a wooden pitchi and buried on the bank to keep cool and make the lilies prosper. Lilies have provided hides for both the hunter and the hunted. Immersing his body in the manner of the lotus bird his nose only projecting above the water the Aborigine would wait for an unwary bird then grab it by the legs.

Below: Rainbow Serpent (with bulbs sprouting Lotus lilies)
after a bark painting from the Gunwinggu.

Jingana the earth mother creator of Western Arnhem Land gobbled up all the human-animal creatures one day in a fit of anger then threw them up in their present forms.
In time she laid two large eggs which hatched to a son, NGALJOD, and a daughter NGALGUN-BURIMAIMI. Like his mother Ngaljod had the body of a snake with the chest bone of an emu. His feathered headdress is worn by Aborigines in ceremonial honour of this Rainbow Serpent to ensure a balance of wet and dry seasons so that food such as water lilies will be plentiful. He creates clouds by shooting vapour into the sky then pierces them with his forked tongue

to empty in torrential rain. His tongue flickers across the sky as lightning and he growls thunder. His sister, Ngalgun-Burimaimi, was more like a fish with a human head.

The large cupped leaves of the Lotus Lily (Nelumbo nucifera) sometimes reach higher than its deep carmine flowers, distinctly different from the giant water lily.

The contented honking and grunting increases as more and more waterfowl return to accept us into their habitat. Camouflaged by the dappled shade of giant paperbarks I sketch w minimal movement. That mouse-like squeak from a bird is odd but stranger still to watch it walk on water. So this is the Christbird locals talk about. Also known as a lilytrotter, though more generally as the jacana or lotus bird, it stalks on longish legs across the lagoon, the long fine toes and nails spanning the large lily pads. Though its feet are not webbed it can swim under water and stay under for a considerable time breathing through the nostrils in its bill protruding above water like a periscope. When brooding this bird is aggressive against predators. In retreat it has the unique ability to pick up small chicks and eggs with its wings.

The chicks are crazily fluffed
with absurdly lanky legs
miraculously created
for this special habitat.

As though painted by a child
at Easter the lotus bird's eggs nest at water level
on a leafy platform that is partly immersed
when the parent bird sits!

To distract predators from the nesting site
the jacana will display by flopping and
floundering as though
with a broken wing.
At high pitch
of excitement its red
comb changes to yellow.
Both parents care for the chicks.
With their perky little tails
flicking as they step from leaf
to lily pad building extra nests
for emergencies such as sudden
flooding in the violent "wet."

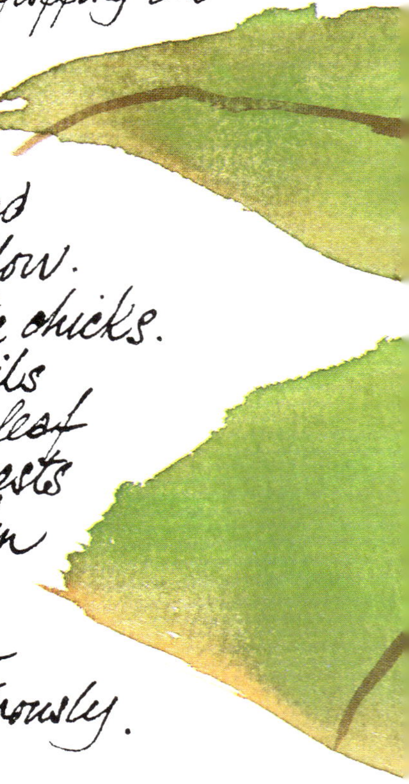

A hedonist, the lotus bird luxuriates in the sun
lying on it's side and stretches its long legs voluptuously.

Irediparra gallinacea
wings are spurred
trails legs in flight
length about 23cms.
females are larger than males.

A scre-e-e-ech rasps the 'soft bat' night — cave or masked owl? Same bird and both sound sinister; dropped off to sleep again with the mildly disturbing yet comforting thought that owls are moth-like to feel.

A slash of dawn across the billabong as a pair of pelicans swish the lilied surface; fishing, perhaps courting away from the flotilla. In unhurried serenity they satisfy their curiosity about intruders like ourselves but paddle faster and lift their bulk in what appears to be a near impossible take off; yet in flight the demands of nature and those of art are held in equipoise. Airline pilots report pelicans flying at 3000m above sea level and this is not surprising for a species which has been perfecting the art for some 30 or 40 million years. According to research into fossil remains these prehistoric birds have changed little in all that time.

Chewing barbecued chops last evening with the Aboriginal household of Bob Randall, public-relations man who cushions any conflict between traditional owners and Pan Continental's plans to mine their land, we met two local painters. When Bob escorted them to another room I stayed talking with the women but his wife Lorraine said I should join the men "... in this house we do not join in men's business." The business we talked was art — the recurring themes of the snake as snake and as the supreme spirit Rainbow Serpent — of the snake as symbol in the Garden of Eden — of the Lightning man sometimes depicted as woman and of other anthropomorphous spirits with sexual duality. But talk was reduced to my monologue punctuated occasionally by a puzzled nod from the unenlightened Bob. The artists seemed reluctant to discuss their work — perhaps in attitude they were agreeing that little in art is communicated through words. The only telling comment on a painting is another painting. How can we discuss imagination — the soul's thought or perhaps the shadow of some impalpable truth? The older of the two, Peter Parmanitbal, is inscrutable, dignified, oriental in his 'otherness', a white beard whispy in the deep furrows of his black handsome features. Even more taciturn was the younger Jim with the profile of an outlier, lower lip protruding like a rock shelter.

Though he spoke little of bark painting technique beyond. "... put one white, two red lines, two black over," Peter promised to demonstrate the art of painting on rock — tomorrow in the morning.

This morrow we collect him at Mudginberri where he lives just beyond the station buildings and cattle yards in the concrete Aboriginal quarters, separate in his own iron gunyah with a young wife, who smokes a big pipe, and their ten children, the youngest a toddler. This child and a four year old girl Peter put in the back of the truck with a kerosene tin of red and yellow ochre chunks and lime clay, grinding rock, several stems of a bamboo-like grass for brushes, broader ones made from slices of stringy bark (the outer bark at one end teased until the fibres are exposed), sticks of charcoal and tobacco tins for water and resin as fixative. Peter directs us back six kilometres short of Ja Ja then off the highway on no marked track through broken bars of sand plunging deep in creek beds with almost sheer 'jump-ups' — two or three kilometres of spine-jolting horror which culminates on a steep rise at a gigantic mushroom of a rock not far from the escarpment. Glad to be out of the hot unstable truck we clamber up to a platform rock at the base of the 'mushroom's' stem. In the shade of this great flowering shelter the eyes adjust from the glare to take in paintings of birds, fish and beings, stick figures of the Mimi. Most impressive are two largish figures, harlequin decorated bodies in ceremonial dance, red and yellow ochres damaged by seepage and plastered with hornets' mud nests but the white linear images remain clear. As is their way image is painted over image.

Peter considers three sites before selecting the surface for his painting. First one is too dark, the second is the wrong proportion. The third has good light and its roughly diamond shape suits his composition. Frail to the point of bone cracking he grinds the ochres on the flat rock, mixing the coloured powder with a solution of bloodwood resin, and, smiling through large yellowed eyes, he tells of the bombing of Darwin and his army life coast-watching for invading Japanese. As Peter loads and raises a stringy-bark brush to paint on the 'ceiling', quite involuntarily I thrust a finger at a faded but animated image before his brush touches it.

"Old, no good," proclaims Peter. Though he shifts centre a little the ephemeral figure soon disappears under a kangaroo, a snake and a hunter. "How does the hunter kill?" asks Kate. Peter paints a nulla-nulla and two spears explaining, "stone-head spear." "And the snake, what does it mean?" "Him rock snake" obliges Peter with a beautific smile, "good tucker." If the subject had deeper meaning he gave away no clan secrets. From a tobacco tin he dribbles more water on the ochre and mixes it on the flat grinding stone (Before metals were introduced to glitter and rust in the landscape water was carried in tiny canoes of paper-bark). Colour so far is restricted to ochres and black so, "What about white? asks Kate. "Not strong, not eat breakfast," answers

Peter, "you bring tucker? We go for cup of tea — come back and put in white colour." But he calls to the children, throwing stones and playing, to bring some twigs for a small fire. Over this he boils water in another tobacco tin and drops in some lime clay to produce the white and complete his painting. This is one of the last of the rock paintings in the traditional manner and Peter died three years later.

Back at the Ja Ja camp we got them some lunch. Greg, the excellent Chinese cook, warns not to offer them salad, greens they'll throw away, and piles their plates with buns, bread, cake and cold meat. On the way back to Mudginberri we pause by a billabong while Peter selects a stringybark of suitable girth, free of knots and decay, for bark painting. With a machete he cuts a vertical strip, a metre by 30cms, of bark and tears it down. Two horizontal cuts around the trunk, top and bottom of the vertical strip, and Peter eases the bark from the core using the machete as a wedge. "What happens to the tree now?" I ask. "Him die," says Peter as he tosses the cylinder of bark into the truck. Over 40,000 years they killed trees and seasonally burnt the scrub but the landscape bore few scars before recent development. At Mudginberri Peter strips the bark of its rough outer fibre which he fires with dry grass laying the cylinder over it, outer side then inner, to dry out the moisture and make the sheet pliable. Inner surface down on the ground he treads it flat then weights with heavy stones. Within a few days the bark will be flat and ready for trimming and sand-papering — leaves of the Ficus species, such as ficus scobina, provided traditional 'sand-paper'.

Arranging brushes and pigments on a small sheet of bark a palette, Peter takes a prepared sheet, sticks tied top and bottom to prevent warping. He chews the stem of a tree orchid to release the juice which he rubs over the surface of the bark then brushes overall with a solution of red ochre and water. With white, boiled with eucalypt resin, he paints the image of the Lightning man. Selecting a finer brush of grass he paints lines over the figure with red ochre fixed with the orchid juice. Coming back over the figure with fine white lines he causes vibration with cross-hatching. All his strokes are brushed away from his body, his painting hand in fixed position as the other hand turns the bark to control the drawing, the design. With finishing lines of yellow ochre he assures us, "Last ten years." During the day Peter chuckled at the idea of my drawing him while he draws something else.

Ja Ja billabong ↗

← and the arthritic limb of an ancient melaleuca.
More extraordinary is the number of insects and plants, even trees such as the big shady eucalypt Alosyncarpia Ternata, which had not been recorded till recently. In this area field anthropologist George Chaloupka and his companion-adviser Nipper Kapirigi have collected one hundred and fifty odd species of plants, six of which had never been identified.

coot
plumed egret
pied heron
pygmy geese

LARGE EGRET

Egretta alba

Leaning forwards on its long black stilts, its longer-than-body neck stretched out, the large egret suddenly spears its bill into the water. Pincered in the yellow bill a struggling fish is swallowed with an upward thrust of the white bird's head. A loner, this immaculate hunter stalks small aquatic animals — insects, amphibians, crustaceans — in shallow water.

Before the hunting of birds for their feathers was prohibited the large egret's long nuptial plumes were highly prized to adorn ladies' hats.

In breeding season the plumed egret has long, lacy nuptial plumes on its breast and back. (The large egret has them only on its back.) While breeding the plumed egret has a green face, red bill and upper legs. Beyond the breeding season the large and the plumed egrets are look-alikes.

The plumed egret's habits are similar to the large except that it is gregarious and is seen foraging in small groups sometimes in company with the pied heron which is also known as the white-headed egret.

The Alligator rivers floodplain
from Obiri Rock
May 1978

Oenpelli and Ubirr
(Obiri Rock)

— The Aborigines re-adjust to self determination in the old mission at Oenpelli, once the pioneering cattle station of buffalo shooter Paddy Cahill.

— The richness of art found in a labyrinth of caves at nearby Inyalak Hill.

— The grand frieze of fish and superb paintings of the Mimi at Ubirr.

Leaving Ja Ja camp we drive in the dense morning shadow of Mosquito Dreaming, a monumental rock in precarious balance high on the escarpment. Three across the cabin seat is too tight for comfort in this clammy heat. Oenpelli across the East Alligator River is our destination but Bob explains as the truck wallows and lurches through another muddy depression in the red 'highway' we must first deliver supplies promised to an outstation (now called homeland) near Cannon Hill.

Wheel tracks axle deep in mud already baking hard in the sun force the truck to scrub bash detours. Though the bull-bar explodes tall termite mounds to powdered earth and flattens saplings which immediately spring erect steering between solid eucalypts and clumps of screwing pandanus demands energetic driving. The generator and pump are active but the demountable is deserted as we pass the Ranger's outstation and grind on in four-wheel-drive towards a magnificent billabong honking with the contented life of water birds.

Under an overhanging rock decorated with paintings of fish two older women, a grey-haired man, a much younger man and a teenaged girl are camped on a rise of flat sandstone. Dogs of uncertain breed, favouring dingo and whippet, bark as we approach. Scrawny and rarely used for hunting these days they provide warmth at night. Temperature could be gauged by the number of dogs needed for sleeping comfort — in bitter weather we would say this will be a four dog night.

Of the group of Aborigines Topsy is the oldest. Tall and active, topped with a mop of white hair she carries herself with authority. Elizabeth, shorter on spindly legs, smokes the butt of a pipe, hot in her thick lips. Smoke from the camp fire repels the swarming mosquitoes but does not deter the buzz of flies which smother a pile of butchered buffalo meat oozing blood to soon blacken the sandstone. Had they not been cut in slivers the steaks would be already beyond the appetites of the underfed dogs (maggots survive only in thicker cuts).

Mosquito Dreaming – the escarpment at Jaja billabong

No more than twenty-five
summers and this
man's torso is an ugly
mass of cicatrices —
but he is proud of
them — they are evidence
of stoical ability to
transcend pain.

"Ranger forgot to bring the salt," complains Topsy, slipping a soiled white dress over a less formal one, "you want to camp here tonight, eat with us?"

Kate is keen for the experience, to learn more about their ways, their weaving, their cooking — but that forbidding pile of bleeding and blown buffalo! Traditionally the meat would have been preserved by cooking soon after killing. The Aborigine's increasing, unhealthy dependence upon introduced food was expressed by these women in their need to buy from the supermarket at Oenpelli. They bemoaned their lack of ready cash but Topsy remembered her pension cheque was due.

Charlie, the older man, wanted

a lift to Mudginbarri, in the opposite direction, but decided to pack his swag and ride with us to Oenpelli. Faraway in a dream he rolled up a sleeping dog with his simple belongings in a grey blanket, unaware of it till the dog yelped.

From the camp they could almost reach into the billabong, a huge 'supermarket', and take without charge all manner of wild fowl, barramundi, crayfish and turtles, waterlilies and other edible vegetation — a balanced and varied diet. They retain their tradition of sharing and that includes money. Bob explains that in family all things are shared equally. Family is not simply joined by blood. There are 'skin' brothers, sisters, cousins — all adopted and living in a mutually assisting community. This reflects the 'wantok' (one talk) way of life in Papua New Guinea where we had known a white man married to a black woman obliged to share his income with her endless relatives and their wantoks.

A collection of Aboriginal 'family' clans cannot be called a tribe because their clans are formed around this complex system of skin-ship wherein 'name' is more fundamental than blood. Ancestor spirit and totem kinship inhabit the 'name' and such relationship is of supreme importance and extends for all time regardless of distance or length of separation from the clan. 'Name' sacred objects and emblems, extending to body decoration are the clan secret. Their belief is clan collective not personal as expressed in Christianity. This belief in a system of spirits is given form in totemic symbol which is imbued with meanings and taboos. Things and places associated with the totems possess the spirit. The creature or plant chosen by the clan as totem is each member of the clan

A cacophony of oo-oo-urkk from the billabong draws attention to hundreds of ibis — the straw-necked is the most common of three species found in Australia. When courting the pair develop red patches on either side of the breast and to the rear of the eyes. The mating birds bow with wings partly spread then preen one another. In pecking attack the "straw" neck feathers are ruffled aggressively.

(*Threskiornis spinicollis*)
length – 700mm.

hence each is himself the sacred totem. If they deified any particular thing it would be the clan itself. The Rainbow Serpent in its many forms being the most ancient known of religious images the Aboriginal spiritual system has to be the World's longest living religious culture.

Of an Aboriginal-European union Bob Randall was born at Ayers Rock. As a youngster he was taken from his people in the Centre to a mission on Croker Island off the far north coast, victim of Government strategy to separate children of mixed blood from their Aboriginal families and clan ritual so they could be educated for assimilation into European society.

In fear of Japanese landing after the bombing of Darwin in the Second World War the Croker Island

mission was evacuated. With two young women to care for and guide them the children were put ashore on the mainland near the mangrove-choked mouth of the South Alligator River. With meagre supplies and no further help from the authorities the children faced a long and tortuous walk south in search of civilisation. As a displaced person Bob is perhaps more conscious of clan 'skin-ship' than blood kinship.

With the women around the fire Kate remarks on a woven lid on top of a steaming iron pot and asks Topsy to weave similar objects as place mats. With a coal from the fire Kate draws a circle on the flat sandstone to indicate size; selecting dye colours from a basket on the rock is natural because a large slab of sandstone serves as our dining table in Sydney. Ten dollars a mat for ten mats is agreed and ten days later the first mat perfect in proportion and subtle in colour is produced. As encouragement Kate pays an advance but Topsy completed no more. Each year and seven years later I still remind Topsy we want the other nine mats and each time she looks at me equivocally and says, 'Making other things now— come and see.' The women are adept weavers; in this case from pandanus they soak fine strips of the leaves with plants of the dye colour required. 10 or 15 strips are formed into a length. Other strips are stitched in criss-cross to bind the mass together and one coil is bound around another.

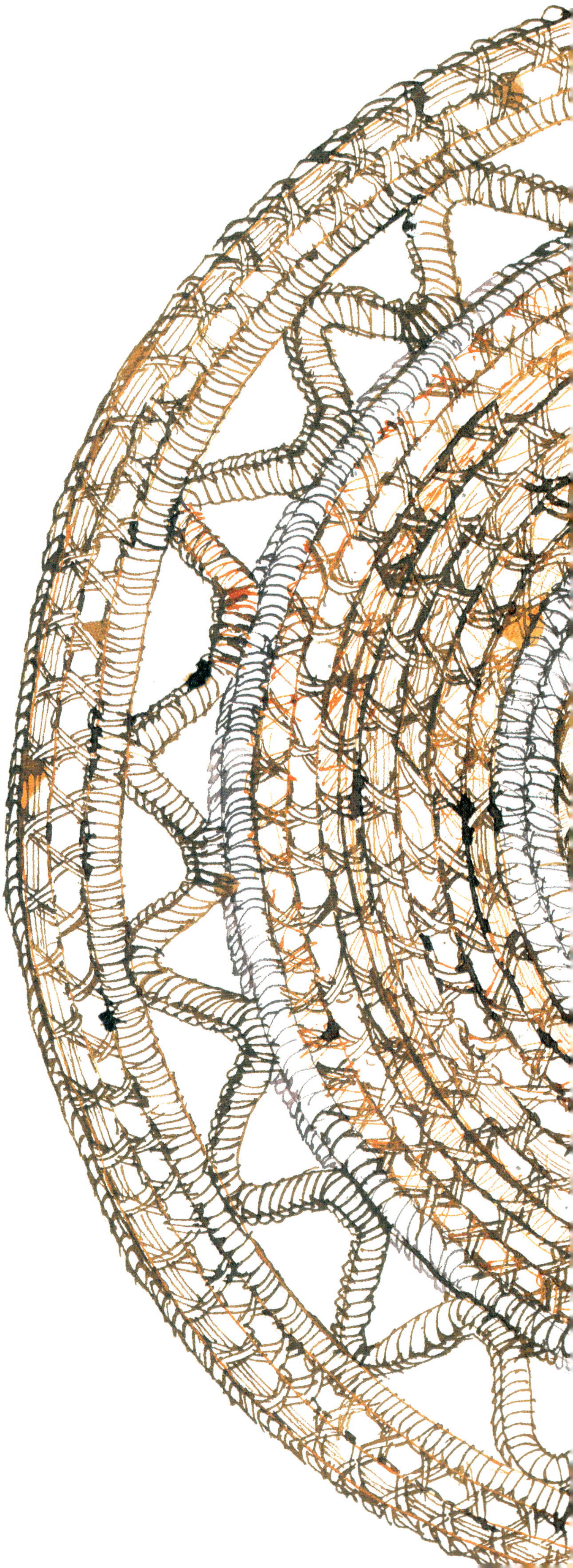

Dilly bags for the occasion and for domestic use.

This 'biting bag' containing a finger bone of the deceased is clenched defiantly between the teeth of a dancer in mortuary ceremony among the Yoingu group.

Also from the Milingimbi area a sacred dilly bag of woven pandanus decorated with parrot feathers. It contains bits and pieces relating to ceremony and is worn by a man or hung from a tree during ritual performance.

And dilly bags used by both men and women for food gathering and carrying personal things. Made of vegetable dyed pandanus fibre some are woven tight to carry water.

52 cms
47 cms
80 cms
Painted and
woven baskets.
Alligator Rivers.

In flood the plains are simplified as a town is under snow. Out here one can understand the pantheist belief in the unity of nature. It is a mass, a whole. It paints itself — outline and detail are left out, volume and gravity unimportant, spatial relations unsettled. Yet, rising out of the vapour near a boiling lagoon of 'red lilies' an outlier of sandstone will not be denied. It towers above us sheer, weathered in evocative form. Pitting in the surface between one and two hundred metres from the base Bob says was caused by spears. It was a target range for throwing practice used by hunters perhaps in competition. Paintings below protected by overhanging rock indicate that this has been a site for ritual.

As Kate spoke with the women about food gathering Bob drew me aside in conspiratorial manner to a more secluded spill of rocks. Access to this gallery up an almost vertical conglomerate ensures its secrecy. In a crevice are human bones and beer cans. I comment, "Sacrilege." Bob shrugs his shoulders, "Long time ago, long forgotten. When the bones of an Aborigine are clean and sun-bleached they are wrapped in bark and placed in final rest by the closest relative, who visits the burial site frequently until it is felt that the spirit is contented. Having separated himself from the deceased the mourner is once more a complete person. And these paintings must not be seen by women." The Mimi style here is similar to that in paintings we had seen nearer Oenpelli but the images are more explicit: a spindly though dynamically rendered female figure with wide and extended vulva and a male with an unwieldy penis twice his own length, the bodies and organs entwined like the vines and tubers of yams.

The women had dug up some yams in the shade of a clump of pandanus. One of their digging sticks had an iron tip but it did not appear more efficient than the traditional hardwood of the other. Climbing among the pandanus the wiry stems with heart-shaped

Target Rock 1979.

'Yam people': Anthropomorphic yams. After a Mimi rock painting at Djuwarr, Deaf Adder Creek.

leaves guide the gatherer down to the tubers, at times as deep as fifty centimetres in the earth. Some species are eaten raw after washing, others require processing to rid them of poisonous matter. Those with acrid taste Aboriginal women cut and soaked preferably in running water for several hours. Topsy and her friend will then boil the yams but not so long ago they had not the metal pots for this. The more fibrous tubers they would have baked in the coals then washed before straining off the fibrous matter, repeating the process in many changes of water before eating. It has the flavour of potato though a bit waxy. The mess was never stored because of fermentation in humid heat.

Yams (Dioscorea) and taro (colocasia esculenta) have long been cultivated in Asia, Africa and America. Though in the Wahgi valley of Papua New Guinea's central highland gardening of these farinaceous plants dates back nine thousand years their cultivation was not known to Aborigines. Perhaps in the vast natural gardens of the Kakadu it was necessary only to leave the very top of the tuber attached to the tendril in the ground to grow again.

The Washkuk hills of Ambunti on the Sepik River are the centre of a yam cult. To the dancing of female spirits bamboo flutes, water-drums and conch shells haunt the nights before planting and harvesting. Basket-weave masks are worn and wooden masks carved with long noses and tongues, symbols of fertility, are stuck in the gardens in an appeal to ancestor spirits to provide a bumper crop. 'Yam people' painted on rocks many thousands of years ago and today's bark paintings of yams are evidence of a continuing cult in Arnhem Land. Taking into account other New Guinean influences such as painted skulls, string figures, wooden gongs and painted grave posts it seems reasonable to assume that before the 'bridge' which linked the two countries was finally washed away 6,500 years ago the yam cult was shared by both peoples.

At many ceremonial grounds in Western Arnhem Land yams are inextricably involved in early Mimi paintings of anthropomorphic beings. These reflect the Aboriginal cosmology of man and his environment — all creatures, all beings spiritual and corporeal share a oneness. Sacred rangga resembling tubers with feathered string to simulate the vines and foliage of yams were buried to stimulate growth. Cautionary legends about poisonous foods and greed are perpetuated in song. The Gunwinggu sing of two women who died immediately they dug a sacred yam.

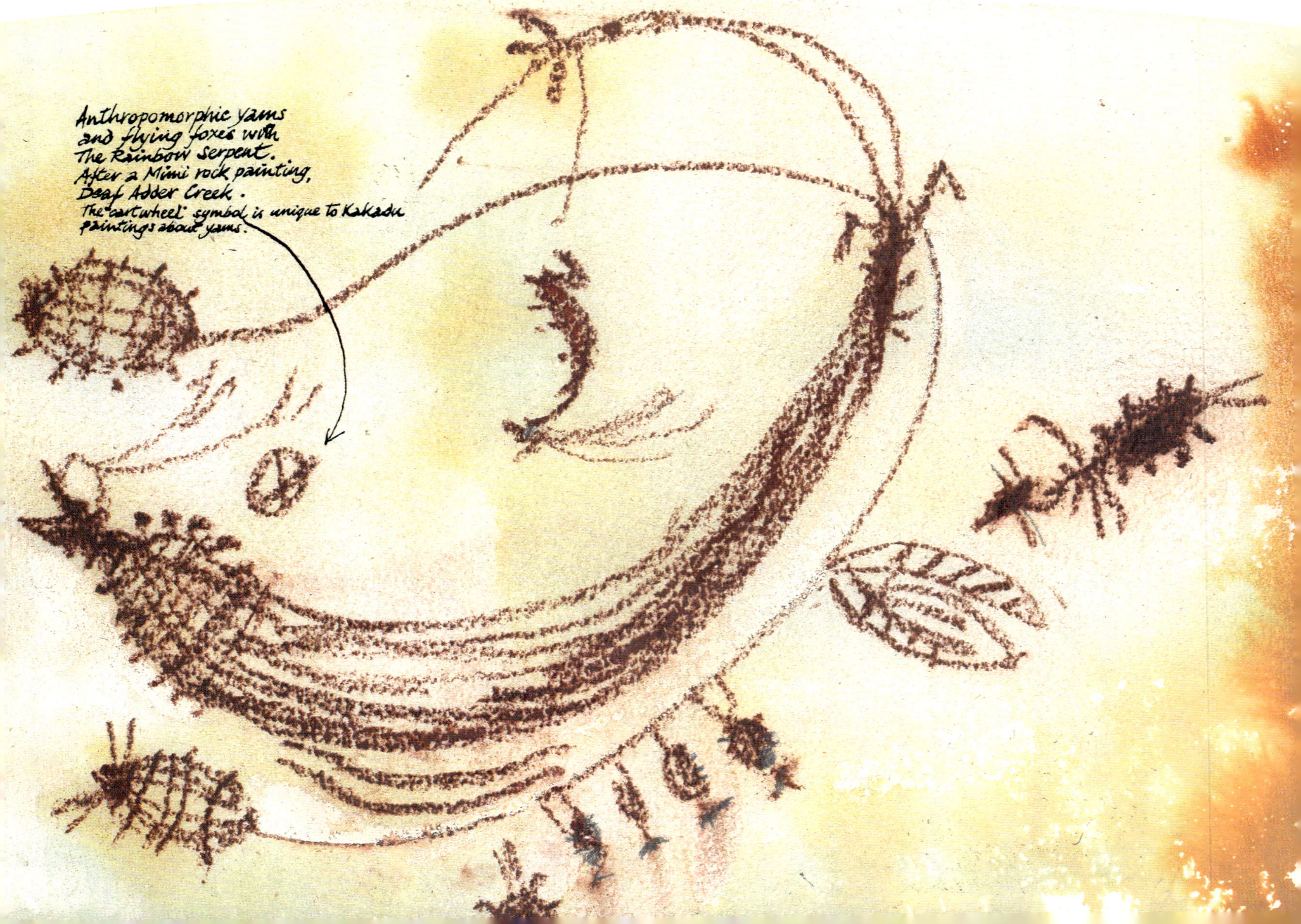

Anthropomorphic yams and flying foxes with The Rainbow Serpent. After a Mimi rock painting, Deaf Adder Creek. The 'cartwheel' symbol is unique to Kakadu paintings about yams.

Mostly, people rely on bees to collect and process their nectar into honey. But Aborigines, along with insects, honeyeater birds, bats and pygmy possums, gathered nectar, a sugar solution in the lower part of blossoms, from its source in certain wild species. Even today they will suck the flowering whiskers of banksia "bottle brush" or soak it in water to make a pleasant drink. Knowledge of species is important — there have been reports of nausea and headaches resulting from overdose.

Ludwig Leichhardt, on his Port Essington expedition observed Aborigines washing nectar from Melaleuca blossoms and noted in his journal: "We gathered some blossoms of the drooping tea-tree, which were full of honey, and, when soaked, imparted a very agreeable sweetness to the water." On another occasion after tasting the fruit of the small Grewia shrub, known as emu-berries and enjoyed by Aborigines, he wrote: "Whilst walking down by the lagoon, I found a great quantity of ripe Grewia seeds, and, on eating many of them, it struck me that their slightly acidulous taste, if imparted to water, would make a very good drink; I therefore gathered as many as I could, and boiled them for about an hour; the beverage which they produced was at all events the best we had tasted on our expedition; and my companions were busy the whole afternoon in gathering and boiling the seeds."

Aborigines applied crushed Grewia leaves to ease pain such as toothache.

On further experiment in survival crossing the Northern Territory Leichhardt recorded: "There was another small tree, the branches of which were thickly covered with bright green leaves; it had round inferior fruit, about half an inch in diameter, which was full of seeds: when ripe, it was slightly pulpy and acidulous, and reminded me of the taste of the coarse German rye bread. In consequence of this resemblance, we called the little tree the Bread tree of Lynd. I ate handfuls of this fruit without the slightest inconvenience." Just as well because the Aboriginal remedy for diarrhoea was large clay or mud pills or a handful of ant bed. Chewing an orchid bulb was said to be more effective — painters used this juice to bind their earth pigments. Resulting constipation could be alleviated by eating the oily liver of stingray, boiled.

The blossoms
of many grevillia
provide eatable
honey-like nectar but
caution is advised. For Aborigines
each plant has a dreaming; each is recorded
in song-cycles which remind of where the food is to be found,
the time to collect it, how to prepare and cook it and,
warning of the danger of poison, the periods when
a plant may not be eaten.

Head, neck + tail
bronze-green – black
wing feathers — legs vermilion
black + white

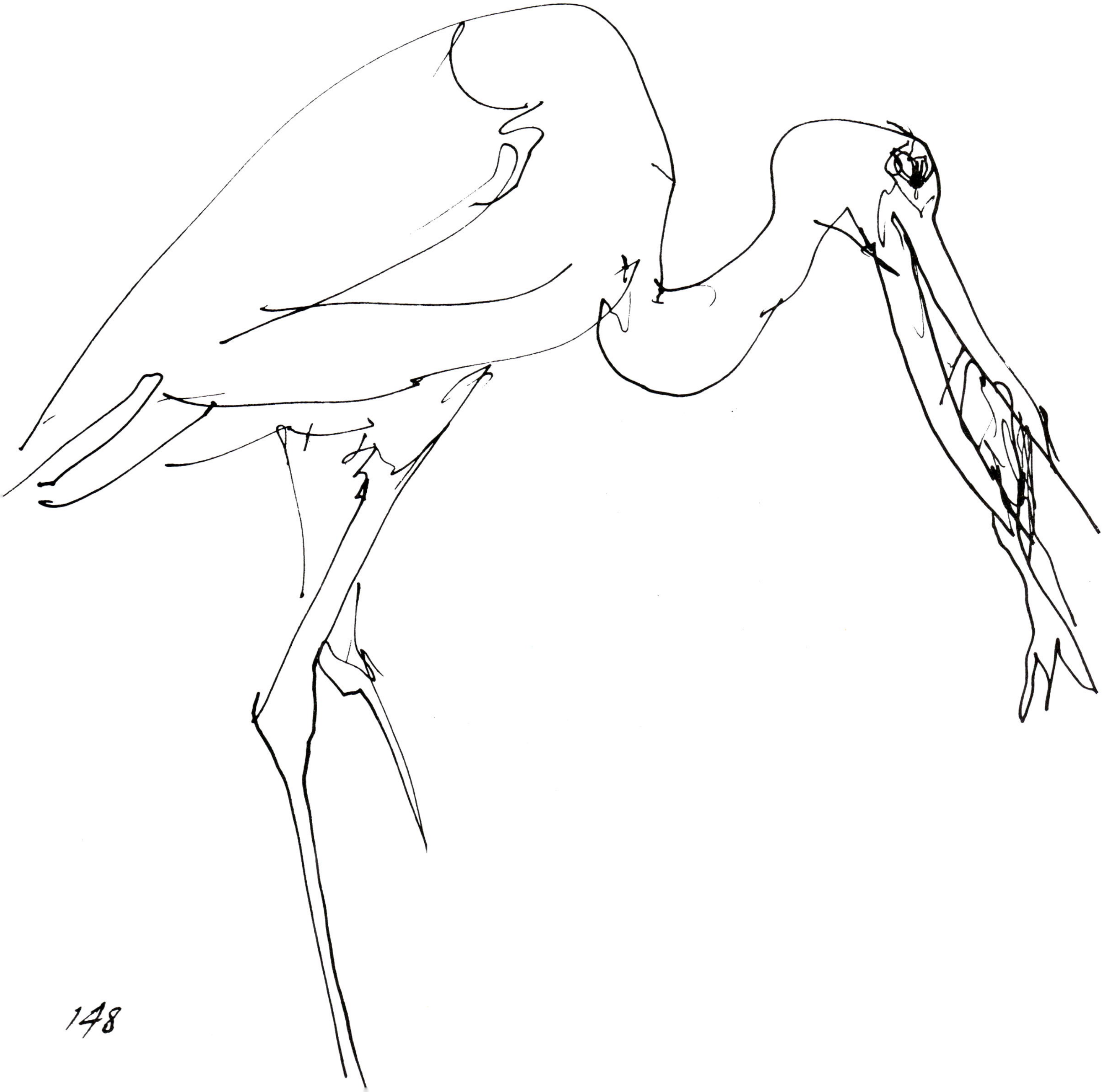

A loner, the jabiru stalks through shallow water jabbing at fish, frogs, crabs, reptiles and carrion with its large, powerful bill. Spotting active prey it takes a few disjointed strides before snapping the food and swallowing with a backward jerk of the head. Even when moving in a small family group, a rare sight, these storks hunt independently of one another.

The weird and varied architecture of termitaria creates a fantasy world. Each mound is a city with a population of about a million. In the Gulf country these 'cities' rise to heights of eight metres. Termite society is structured. The workers are mostly blind, wingless and sexless. They build and repair, gather food and keep the pantries stocked, groom the queen and tend her eggs and offspring.

Suffering the same physical inadequacies the soldiers defend the queen and guard the foraging workers. Their heads are powerfully armoured and equipped with a forehead gland which discharges an irritant at enemies. The exclusive reproduction unit, the queen, lays about 30,000 eggs a day.

from a rock painting at Mount Gilruth.

Chewing wood as food the workers use it also as building material bound with their excreta and cemented with saliva.

Unpalatable as it may seem Aborigines eat a handful of termite mound with a fistful of echidna — a combination like a paper of fish and chips. Though termites are staple food for the echidna its own flesh when cooked is rich in flavour similar to pork. Aborigines burn off the echidna's spines before skinning and gutting. With a belly filled with hot stones the roast is placed in the open fire and covered with earth to bake in its own juices.

The magnetic termite constructs relatively thin mounds which point north-south so their broad sides face the sun morning and afternoon and only the narrow edge is exposed to the fierce mid-day temperature. This form of solar heating provides maximum drying and warming benefits for the termitaria. Humidity is maintained at near saturation point and temperature varies little.

The rock is ash grey now the sun has turned off the blow torch and an echidna pokes its exploratory nose from a narrow crevice at the base. Well camouflaged in this spiky landscape it tracks through the yellow grass like a war machine from some other planet. Surrounded by masses of food, productivity is high in fantastic termitaria, the echidna soon breaches a mound with its' clawed forepaws and tubular snout and extends a long tongue into the busy galleries. Adhering to the sticky saliva termites are drawn into the echidna's mouth and masticated between horny pads on its palate. Moving in for closer study we disturb this evening meal and the echidna curls in a defencive ball with radiating spines. On softer ground it would have dug in and disappeared like a sinking ship.

Just now, July – August, is the mating season. We have seen four and five males pursuing the one female.

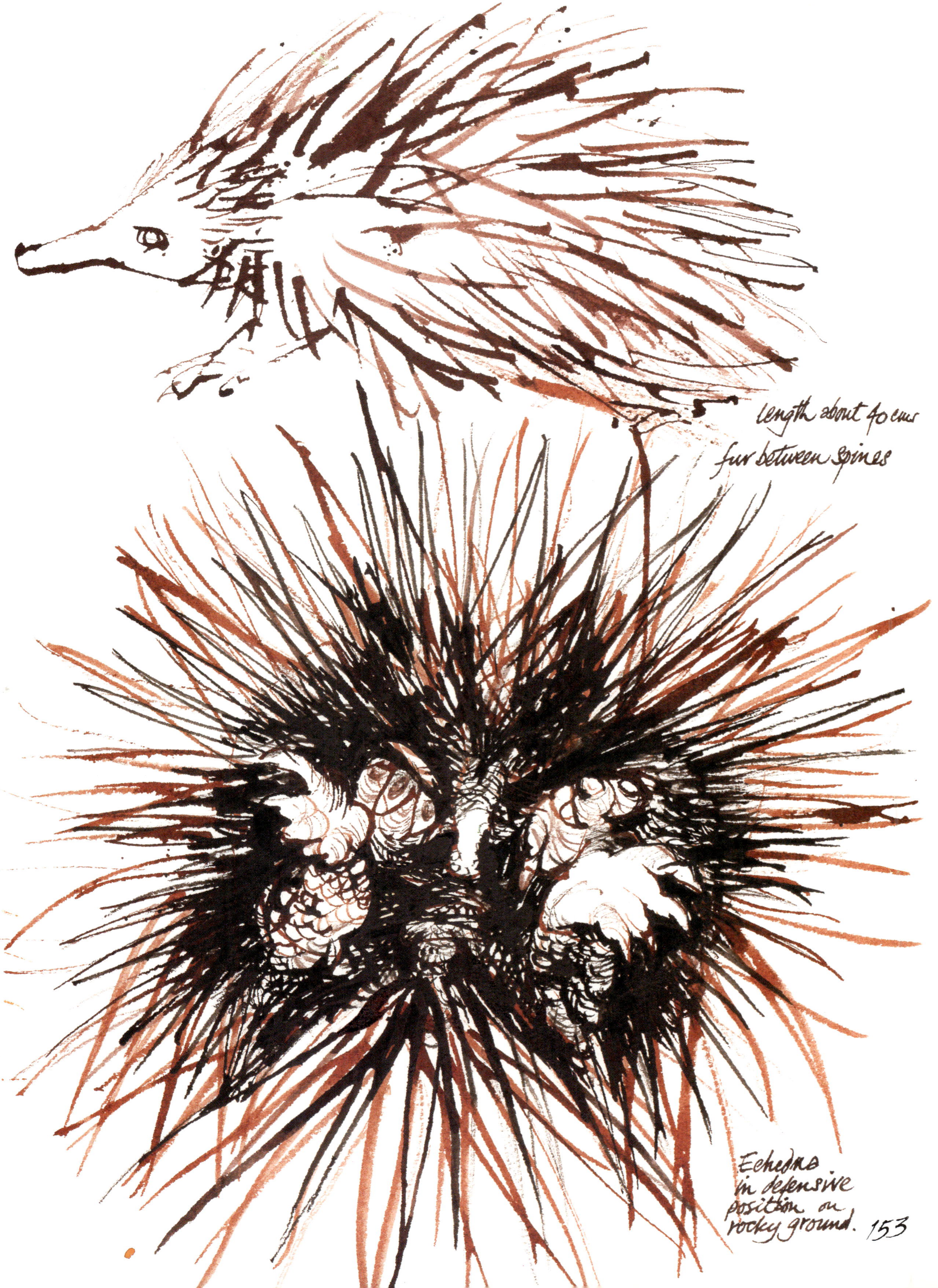
length about 40 cms
fur between spines
Echedna
in defensive
position on
rocky ground.

The escarpment hovers like a protective phantom over the rich food plain, separated from it by a wide ribbon of mist at the base. On the barren plateau above animated rocks suggest prehistoric activity. What has the appearance of a cairn for ancient rites draws me to closer inspection. As I prepare to jump a fissure two metres wide Kate holds me and we look deep, down three hundred metres or more — that experience has triggered many vertiginous nightmares for us both.

Ludwig Leichhardt was best equipped to describe the Arnhem Land plateau. The first Europeans to penetrate this barrier his expeditionary party camped nearby. His journal reads: "…. most disheartening, sickening view over a tremendously rocky country. A high land, composed of horizontal strata of sandstone, seemed to be literally hashed, leaving the remaining blocks in fantastic figures of every shape; and a green vegetation, crowding deceitfully within their fissures and gullies, and covering half of the difficulties which awaited us on our attempt to travel over it." Down on the Alligator rivers plain he wrote more enthusiastically: "…. a passage between the lagoons, and entered into a most beautiful valley, bounded on the west, east and south by abrupt hills, ranges and rocks rising abruptly out of an almost treeless plain clothed with the most luxuriant verdure, and diversified by large Nymphae lagoons, and a belt of trees along the creek which meandered through it." This gentle landscape which embraced Leichhardt's party and enabled them to recover from the hell above is now called Oenpelli. In those days it was known as Gunbalanya by the Gunwinggu, their way of pronouncing Unbalanj as the Mengerr language group called it, and Oenpelli is our attempt to spell it.

Beyond parties of the explorers John McDouall Stuart in 1862 and John McKinlay 1865-66 few Europeans knew this plain until the buffalo shooters of the 1880s and 1890s. Buffalo had been shot-out in the Oenpelli area by the turn of the century when Paddy Cahill established a cattle station here, taking out a licence in 1906. The landscape was unchanged and the Cahills were living happily alongside the many healthy and helpful Aborigines when Baldwin Spencer visited in 1912. In 'Wanderings in Wild Australia' Spencer wrote: "…. luxuriant flats stretch back to a series of picturesque rocky ranges, running away for miles north and south. It is really a beautiful place, especially in the early morning when the Ranges, catching the soft pink light, rise out of the mists that lie along the flats and valleys, and again at evening, when they are richly coloured with intense purples, blues, greens and reds. There are beautiful clumps of trees on the margin of the lagoon not far away from the house, and altogether it is much the most beautiful spot that I have seen in the Territory..... It was just like an English meadow, with luscious green grass...... We had before us a sinuous line of thirty or forty bronze-coloured, lithe-limbed natives, following a trail through the rich green of the swamp grass and herbage, bright here and there, with yellow flowers and purple lilies on little water-pools;"

The grass is no longer green. In 1978, our first visit, the swamp is still here but denuded of 'luxuriant verdure'. Rather than an 'English meadow' this could be a street in Calcutta. Though birds continue to use it the 'nymphal lagoon' appears defiled. In this now un-Christian setting the mission compound is a dustbowl pounded by hundreds of bare feet — in the 'wet' mud oozes between the toes. This suffocating treeless mudflat supports many structures, flimsy shelters patched with thin plywood

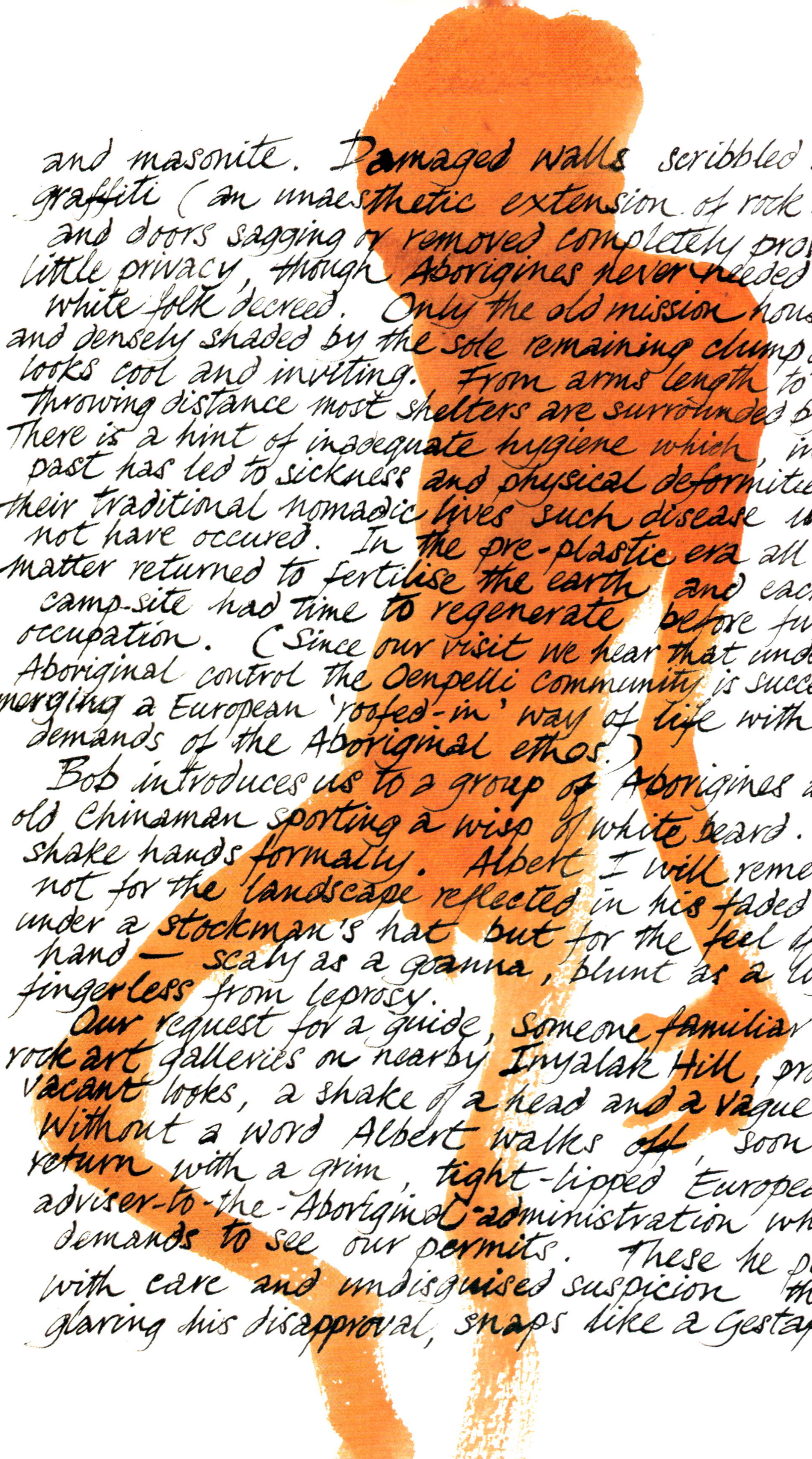

and masonite. Damaged walls scribbled with graffiti (an unaesthetic extension of rock art?) and doors sagging or removed completely provide little privacy, though Aborigines never needed it till white folk decreed. Only the old mission house, fenced and densely shaded by the sole remaining clump of trees, looks cool and inviting. From arms length to casual throwing distance most shelters are surrounded by litter. There is a hint of inadequate hygiene which, in the past has led to sickness and physical deformities. Living their traditional nomadic lives such disease would not have occured. In the pre-plastic era all discarded matter returned to fertilise the earth and each camp-site had time to regenerate before further occupation. (Since our visit we hear that under Aboriginal control the Oenpelli community is successfully merging a European 'roofed-in' way of life with the demands of the Aboriginal ethos.)

Bob introduces us to a group of Aborigines and an old Chinaman sporting a wisp of white beard. We shake hands formally. Albert I will remember not for the landscape reflected in his faded eyes under a stockman's hat but for the feel of his hand — scaly as a goanna, blunt as a log — fingerless from leprosy.

Our request for a guide, someone familiar with the rock art galleries on nearby Inyalak Hill, produces vacant looks, a shake of a head and a vague smile. Without a word Albert walks off, soon to return with a grim, tight-lipped European adviser-to-the-Aboriginal-administration who demands to see our permits. These he peruses with care and undisguised suspicion then, glaring his disapproval, snaps like a Gestapo officer,

"These are not valid. Two signatures are needed, not one. You must face the council. And no photographs are to be taken around here." We do not carry cameras.

Morning heat builds in the concrete council chambers, a building no more impressive than the domestic quarters. A rather diffident black president lost in the gloom behind a school desk gets to his feet slowly when he sees Kate to upend a chair, spilling a litter of magazines and papers on to the floor then had one of his men clear a seat for me. Reason for visit stated on my permit, 'to study rock art and to sketch the landscape', is queried by the president, "What is landscape?" "Land forms," I explain, "The shape of hills, the colour of billabongs," and show him a sketch book. Two blacks shadowing the doorway's dingy light move in to look over the president's shoulder as he turns the pages. Still pondering he comments defensively, "You should have another signature." Kate asks, "Would you be able to sign?" He does so, large and in red ink, saying, "You show this to police if they ask."

Under mid-1970s policy of self-determination control of Oenpelli was handed over to Aborigines by the Anglican Church Missionary Society. The mission had been established in 1925 on the site the Government had purchased from Paddy Cahill to form an agricultural research station (a brave but foolhardy attempt to produce butter from cows discontented in a hot climate). Cahill as buffalo shooter and cattle station owner had won the respect and confidence of Aborigines to the extent that ten clans were drawn to socialise at Oenpelli. From these a selection of personalities suitable for potential conversion was made later by missionaries with the Goverment accepted idea of restructuring Aboriginal society.

A now cooperative council has difficulty finding a guide to show us the art of Inyalak. Few whites and it seems fewer blacks have visited the hill in recent years. Finally a man working in 'hygeine' volunteers — he had been brought up in the cave shelters of Inyalak

Cormorants on
the look-out
and drying
their wings
after diving
for fish

some twenty five years back.
A few kilometres from Oenpelli we parked the truck at the base of Injalak which, with the hills of Arrguluk and Nimbabirr, overlooks and abounds the billabong and settlement. As we follow our guide through head high yellow grass with a tough cutting edge and hidden stumbling rocks on several false trails it becomes increasingly obvious that our guide has not revisited the scene of his childhood for some time. Literally cooked for an hour in fruitless search on this steep

slope we express our doubt but the guide assures us he lived here with three hundred people though has not been back. We retreat to the truck which is better equipped to bash through the grass and pandanus. Blocked by rock we are on foot again — barefoot because the climb is precipitous for a hundred and more metres. Then the agony and earlier frustrations inflicted by a petty bureaucrat are forgotten under a great sheltering rock, the richly decorated foyer

of a labyrinth of galleries. Images of magpie geese peep through the forms of wallabies and other species of food animals but superimposed fish and turtles dominate. Distinctive painting styles are brushed one over another from early stick figures to the later Mimi fleshed-out, vivacious 'running girls' (much smaller than I had expected), large spirit beings — varied representations of the Rainbow Serpent, and polychrome Xray paintings. To complete this rock museum's history of Aboriginal art there are excellent examples of culture contact art — figures of Europeans with rifles. (Back along the roadside near Oenpelli is a convincing painting of Cahill's boat "Polly" and in shelters across the East Alligator there are depictions of other vessels including Macassan praus, painted probably by people from the coast known to visit inland clans).

But here at Inyalak vital little Mimi figures pop up in impossible places, well above a painter's reach and in crevices so narrow it would seem possible

only had the artist been equipped with a periscope. In the narrow tunnels which link the shelters are 'magic' paintings — copulating couples, Xray bodies of women showing foetal growth and others suckling babies; most common are those of women with multiple arms and heads of the Rainbow Serpent or a hawk, frequently up-ended with catfish bones or stingray nails protruding from their elongated and grossly enlarged vulvas.

The catacomb's niches with scattered human remains and the masses of discarded shells, animal bones and ashes in the shelters point to seasonal occupation over thousands of years.

Roughly two kilometres long by

one across this residual is cleft in deep chasms. In the cool, filtered light of a central cave, once a busy congregational and living area with fires projecting shadows into the vaulted dome and animating walls of painted multiple imagery, an emphatic sense of spirituality commands silence; a spirituality foreign to us yet recalling the much later Christian religiosity of the great cathedrals of Europe, particularly that of Barcelona with its candle blackened walls built over Roman catacombs.

Out in the glare on top of the two hundred metre 'dome' we look over the leached-out flood plains from escarpment to the East Alligator River. The sky claims its blue from waterholes in grass already yellowed and the rich brown soil bakes paler. Between river and hill thirty two rock art galleries have been recorded but none as interesting as Inyalak itself.

The Kakadu Experience 1979-83

Seen against the squalid backdrop of Oenpelli the shelves of tinned food in the supermarket glitter like decoration on a Christmas tree. No fresh food is displayed. Originally run by the mission the astronomical, higher than Darwin prices should provide handsome profit. It has no liquor licence but the Border Store just seven kilometres away does and many a pension cheque is squandered there. Resulting violence caused the more responsible Aborigines to petition for revocation of the licence. This had the support of Pan Continental chairman Tony Grey whose staff conscientiously cleared the highway of offending beer cans, particularly in the vicinity of the company's model research camp. Later in 1978 the Department of Aboriginal Affairs purchased the Border Store and the licence was cancelled, only to be granted closer to home at the Oenpelli Social Club. At least the incidence of road accidents decreased. Many an early morning Cahill's Crossing had been blocked by trucks which had failed to steer the narrow concrete causeway over the East Alligator a few hundred metres from the Border Store. On one occasion we stopped by a truck caught in the branches of a tall tree. Seated on a rock nearby the Aboriginal driver clearly believed the vehicle had an independent spirit as he explained, "Him goanna — climb tree."

As we drive past Red Lily Lagoon a pair of Pelicans hover with awesome serenity, their great bodies impossibly airborne.

Closer to Cahill's Crossing we are waved to a standstill by a truckload of merry blacks. The driver asks have we seen Bob. Bob who? The vehicle appears to explode with laughter giving impetus to a shower of beer cans as it regains speed, enveloped in a cloud of red dust.

Only the snake-like head of a crane intent on fish protrudes from the murky surface. Munching a sandwich on the concrete crossing Kate soothes her grass lacerated legs in the tidal East Alligator. The great jaws of a crocodile snap but miss the fisherman's dog. As Kate retrieves her legs a man says, "Sharks come up as far as this."

The shadow of a screw palm stripes a dingo to look like the thylacine it eradicated thousands of years ago. A wild one in fine condition its yellow eyes appraise us, friendly enough though not entirely reassuring. Just off the winding track beyond the Border Store nestling between blue-grey termite mounds and pandanus an iron and sapling gunyah shelters a family of Aborigines. In the grey dust black children tease a listless ginger dog with yellow eyes — pure dingo but pathetically mangy. Their domestication of the dog has proved as disastrous as has European indoctrination of the people themselves.

A few kilometres on we leave the truck in the shadow of Ubirr, more commonly known as Obiri Rock, and brush through waist-high yellow grass to the main gallery. Though well publicised the large mural which dominates the ceremonial ground at the base of Ubirr never loses its element of surprise. The indigo of its overhanging rock intensifies to the point of glowing the sudden pinks and yellows of this collective painting. The Aboriginal artists' palette was limited to earth reds and yellows, black and white but here time weathered images over-painted through thousands of years and the varied surface of the rock itself extend the colour tone. The narrow range of ochres vibrate like music, reaching that pervading yet undefinable quality in nature — its inner power. Colour defies literal and mathematical definition; it has its own syntax. As a wise Oriental commented, "Colour is the language of the listening eye."

The complete significance of any great work of art is contained within itself and is projected on us before we take note of any subject matter. True aesthetic judgement is never calculated — it is immediate and involuntary. Though all manner of things, fish, animals and beings, animate the Ubirr mural it is fundamentally a great abstract composition. Here I am referring to abstraction of idea not of image because it is obvious the subject matter was intended to be representational.

Ubirr mural of Xray fish, turtles and small food animals –

Squinting from direct sun on open plain the eyes adjust slowly to Ubirr's dense shade and the rock's painted images – mostly of fish, barramundi, salmon-tailed and eel-tailed catfish, their bones and internal organs depicted in polychrome Xray style. Though simple forms of this art are found in other parts of the world Xray painting of such complexity and virtuosity is unique to this area of Arnhem Land.

Like most great art of the past Aboriginal rock

dimensions : 2 metres deep by 15 metres long .

art at its peak is a manifestation of spiritual beliefs. Their deeply rooted sense of spirituality and of innovation expressed in widely varied styles place the Ubirr paintings above the cave art of Lascaux and Les Eysées in France, Altimira in Spain and the Bushmen of South Africa. And scientific investigation of the Ubirr occupation site has yielded evidence of man's earliest known graphic expression — 25,000 years b.p. This pre dates the Palaeolithic sites of Europe by 6,000 years.

This reinforces not only the Aborigines' claim to the oldest surviving religion but the longest continuing tradition known to the history of art. Archeological excavation has revealed examples of edge-ground tools, the oldest in* the world yet recorded, and images of the long-beaked echidna, known to have been extinct some 18,000 years, are painted into Kakadu rock.

Local Aborigines say it all began here with the Rainbow Serpent Kalarrbirri the supreme female spirit who remains the major influence in their physical and spiritual world. They refer to the serpent as 'that old lady' and believe the rainbow painting at Ubirr to be a self portrait. A site by the bank of the nearby East Alligator, Kalarrbirri Djobkeng, celebrates her crossing of the river on an epic journey of original creation. The many rivers which snake across Arnhem Land could well be the inspiration for this great totem which is depicted as male, female or hermaphrodite in varied zoomorphic forms. In this way their religion is similar to Pantheism in which gods assimilate themselves into natural forms. For Aborigines all beings and creatures belong to the one social and ritual order. All behaviour is controlled by their belief in pre-existence and reincarnation — their concept of dreaming; one consciousness, the same for dream, for memory and for waking life — time without tense.

Compared with Australia's arid centre and its relative paucity of rock art it seems that the ready availability of food allowed Arnhem Landers endless time for the development of their art. The most talented musicians, Songmen and didjeridu players, and painters were in demand and their services rewarded. Under the great curving frieze on the smooth rock face of Ubirr many important ceremonies were performed to ensure the continuation of rich food sources — the fish, turtles, kangaroos and smaller animals depicted in the mural, a fitting background for gourmets. As they feasted and danced through the cool of the night in a celebration of life and the ancestor heroes who provided all cause and effect became unimportant, all rationalising belonged

* More recently similar tools of comparative age were found in Japan.

to nature.

On the rear wall of a highly decorated open shelter opposite Ubirr's natural temple is the finest example of Mimi art, a style contemporaneous with Xray art. Similar in overall pink and yellow underpainting to the frieze of fish this magnificent mural is alive with lithe figures electric in white pigment, the painted line so fine it appears to have been etched. Each running figure is arrested in individual movement, brandishing spears and throwing them from various woomeras. The spears themselves are evocative of action — some barbed others multi-barbed while others appear to quiver in their simplicity. The subject is the hunt and here the hunters carry goosewing fans, some wear ornaments around their upper arms, dilly bags slung from shoulders and all are keenly observed, brilliantly stylised, dynamic in movement. Overpainted in the centre of the composition are the elongated and ghostly forms of two Namarakan women; string to guide them as they travel at night is looped between their hands.

There is evidence of retouching, thought to be quite recent, but the original possibly dates about the time of the peak of Bushman art in South Africa. The art of both peoples is inextricable from their hunting skills and each worshipped zoomorphic deities. Though much of Bushman art is more realistic in form, their representations of animals particularly are convincingly fleshed out, the art of the Australian Aborigine is more imaginative, more vital, more deeply searched and expressed.

The real subject of this hunting scene mural is, once again, food. When a supply of meat was needed ceremony was essential to ensure a successful hunt. To singing and the rhythm of clap-sticks through the proceeding day the mural would be carefully retouched. During that night ritual was performed in mime — the act of stalking, spearing and killing the prey. On the ground or rock wall an image of the animal to be hunted would be drawn. At the climax of the ceremony spears were thrust into the vital parts of the image. This symbolic enactment psyched the hunters with such

Hunting ceremony — After a rock painting at Ubirr.

confidence that the actual tracking down and killing of the animal was mere formality.

After a rock painting on the ceiling of a cave shelter beside Magela creek on the Arnhem Land plateau.

Opposite: A quill and ink drawing from the female figure in white on the lower part illustrated.

The innovative concept of this female figure is strongly reminiscent of Henri Matisse's late work. Unlike Matisse this local painter felt no need to liberate form from old master doctrine. Knowing nothing of the dilemma of European modernism the Aboriginal artist leans heavily on tradition, his own ancient culture. Yet the painting is modern, vital and flows under such control as we may expect only from a master.

Images with barbs protruding from body joints are connected with sorcery. Here, explains a local Aboriginal, the artist painted many barbs and some in the vagina as a warning to his unfaithful wife.

Aboriginal in ritual dance near Mount Brockman.

← after rock painting of a Mimi in fertility dance ritual on the "ceiling" of a shallow cave shelter near Blue Tongue Dreaming. Sliding into the narrow "jaws" of the cave on my back this Mimi being was less than 60 cms from my nose. The figure's approximate length of 160 cms. caused me to record it in three sections for this reconstruction.

Depicted in elongated form the Mimi are puckish spirit beings. Nipper says they are "other people from long time ago. They run away quick, shy. Some good, some bad, eat man." Paintings of Mimi are thought to be their shadows cast on the rock face as they disappear into caves.

At Barrinjowgen near Maningrida Crusoe Guningbal was the sole creator of this unique Mimi →
For years he has selected a curving branch of softwood to carve a simple helmet shape and tiny arms at one end and short legs at the other, then coated it with red ochre and black and white dots.

In the past such an object would have been made solely for ritual then destroyed when it had served its spiritual purpose. For ritual re-enactment another would be carved to the singing of relevant lyrics. Each carving had to be fine and true to satisfy the supernatural being whose spirit would enter it.

The display of this Mimi carving in museums throughout the world has created a demand for copies but Crusoe continues to make only two each year. These days other artists of the Gunwinggu make this image. The less than sensitive crafting of these mass-produced pieces does point up the integrity of Crusoe's work

ht. 172cms

← Flood plain and hunter.

Nature imitating itself
and art once again:
a monitor cross-
hatched and dotted,
and the flotsam
of receding
flood waters
dangles

Little cave
Eptesicus—
Little Brown Bat
length 50mm
found in colonies of
as many as 500

Deaf Adder Gorge,
Jim Jim and Bilk Bilk mi.

— The treacherous Deaf Adder track, frequently lost then found again, leads to a clear lagoon with white sand beach shaded by twisting pandanus. Towering above escarpment rocks contain inspired rock art.

— In camp at Jim Jim; a creature nocturn.

— The hunter's dilemma: Dave Lindner, protector of crocodiles, lover of buffaloes, kills for conservation and fights to halt mining.

David's blue-black face is lost in the night – only his close-set eyes flicker in the light of the fire. Painter John Firth-Smith says he cant understand most Aborigines but David is well educated. He is a graduate of the Sydney Conservatorium of Music — a concert pianist. Nevertheless he is spooked by the night noises — bats particularly. For protection he wants to climb into Firth's sleeping bag, but the big man says, "You've made a big mistake".

Arnhem Land Long-eared Bat

Pygmy Long-eared Bat

Lesser long-eared bat
(Nyctophilus geoffroyi)

Control is wrenched from my hands as the four wheels in drive settle into the storm gouged tracks which weave between towering rocks along the dirt track to Jim Jim Falls. Past a sign warning off 'unauthorised persons' we branch toward Deaf Adder creek on a lost and found track across a yellow plain cut by washaways four and five metres deep. Driving into these is like stunt flying, nose involuntarily pressed to the windscreen, then body jolted over boulders on the dry bed to be laid way back in near vertical climb. Comfortably spanning the track on top of the jump-up a large goanna rises on hind legs to monitor our approach. "Proper-good tucker," comments George, "like beef." Half brother of Nipper Kaparigi, George is a traditional owner of Deaf Adder Gorge and our passport into this forbidden territory, closed to all but his clan.

We had picked him up early at Butchers Knight camp (sometimes wrongly called Butcher's Knife camp of sanguine legend). Nipper had promised many times to guide us into Deaf Adder — again this morning he claimed forgotten 'other business'. Pulling on a soiled white headband he combed his long grey beard with a plastic fork as he explained seriously, 'pub business.'

That sounded honest enough — his taste for beer is legendary. Last year he had cried off because of an important conference about uranium mining at Ja Ja. Still in the bar at midday I asked him why he hadn't gone. "Want director's fee", he pointed out, "and car with driver."

We had asked Diamond, whose warm enquiring eyes at the one time reflect his soul and search for yours, but he had to attend talks at Ubirr. George, too, was on the board of the Cooinda Motel (owned by the Aborigines though managed by a white couple) but largely because his skin-brother

David was with us he agreed to come along.

Filling the tank at Cooinda seemed to remind George of a fiery thirst which would not be slaked by mild liquid, certainly not from the hose pumping from nearby Yellow Waters. Beer, he demanded — at 8 a.m.

The bar was closed but the rouseabout sweeping the floor sold me half a dozen. George's friendly face clouded, "Dat six can not touch'em side," he complained, "Want case, two case!" Reluctantly I got him one but refused a second on grounds that without refrigeration the beer would soon be undrinkable — already it was 33° Celsius in the shade, probably 43° compressed in the metal cabin. Making sure the beer did not reach those temperatures George and David were merry before we hit the rough country — no doubt it dulled the bumping torture.

The mud is red, at times black, under the yellow grass; impassable in the wet. Webbed strands of vegetation left by receding floods glisten on branches of scrub and close to the track herds of buffalo stare dumbly then stampede.

A cluster of iron and sapling framed canvas structures alongside a pig run George claims as his home. Inside the run with an axe in hand he contemplates for some minutes, gazing at a black boar, then chuckles when I disturb his reverie with suggestions of slaughter. With no immediate wish to push on rests in canvas shade → while I sketch.

The teeth-on-edge scrape of metal against tea-tree to the bashing of the truck over rough ground silences the beer swillers in the back. As more empty cans are tossed to the bush Firth told the culprits it was a bad habit. They seem puzzled so I explain that in the Kakadu Park whites pick them up, but here you litter your own ground, you rubbish your ancestors.

At the base of the escarpment on the cool white sandy beach of a clear lagoon we strip and relax our racked bones. David had been nervously apprehensive on the journey, genuinely spooked by the spirits of the brooding escarpment, the great walls of Deaf Adder Gorge. George had warned repeatedly of great danger awaiting the uninitiated in the lagoon. Now he stands over the kneeling David and appeals to the great ancestor beings in Aboriginal tongue, raising his voice to the sky, wailing, chanting as he places a hand on the novice's head, cupping water in his hands to splash over the behumbled figure. This brief ritual recalls in gesture that of the Baptism of Christ in the painting by Pierro della Francesca in London's National Gallery. In English George proclaims that David will now be safe in the lagoon.

"And the crocodiles," I ask, "did they listen?" He chants again and calls loudly, "No crocodiles here," then with a wink, "only little one". There is a freshwater crocodile, no

more than a metre long, some distance down the opposite beach.

We swim across the lagoon to look at rock paintings of crocodiles — or goannas? George is non-committal about this.

In stifling afternoon heat we penetrate the tall grass and dense scrub along the lower rock faces. George shows us three galleries. One he continues to uncover, digging to clear away the sand and reveal ancient images, he claims is the oldest of all. In his cups at Deaf Adder temperature he declares that people will have to pay lots of money to see these paintings.

Through millenia paintings on the walls of the escarpment have weathered and been overpainted. Each superimposed image has enriched the surface of the rock, a multiplicity of forms creating as many dimensions in depth, fused yet dynamic in impact. Some wise person said, 'The artifact of a true work of art never shows a plane surface'. Much of Aboriginal art is accessible only to the initiated. Instead of painting a subject in three dimensional space they reduce it to symbol. The best of their rock art, frequently figurative, was done for ritual, to please the ancestor not the artist. It concerns daily events but by relating these to ideas of original creation such banalities were interwoven with the cosmos in a human/spiritual concept of the universe.

It has been suggested that the pre-historic paintings in caves at Lascaux in Southern France are of a religious nature: that they have the 'strong sense of decoration which is found in temples, the tombs of Egypt, in sanctuaries of Greece and of Christian religion of the Middle Ages, and that the tracing of an isolated figure is a clue to an overall ceremony. Knowing nothing of European Palaeolithic man's rites one can only guess. I was fortunate to visit Lascaux in the late 1940s before the caves were closed to the public in the early 50s due to rapid deterioration of the paintings. Left with me is a strong impression of keenly observed, superbly drawn animals, full advantage having been taken of a curving rock surface to express a cow's belly in relief. I did not sense imaginative or spiritual qualities in the images even in that womb-like and hallowed atmosphere (even undecorated caves contain an awesome other worldliness). Of style there appeared to be three: matchstick and outline figures, three dimensional images and some geometric pattern.

But Aboriginal artists have used a wide variety of styles to produce a collection of images based on beliefs about many ancestral beings — a virtual pantheon. It seems art and nature constantly imitate one another to stimulate fresh ways of looking at things. Though the rock paintings are frequently esoteric even the spirits of the uninitiated are lifted by the beauty of rendition. "In art," wrote Matisse, "truth and reality begin when one no longer understands." He was referring to the creative act but it is true also of the moment of viewing.

In the shade of a rock painted by his deceased brother George becomes emotional. In consolatory appeal to his ancestors he wails and tears trickle down furrows in the weathered face. Out of control now he threatens to kill for more beer and demands a hundred dollars for each gallery he has shown us. I manage to hold his eye with what is hoped to be a kind and sincere look and his mood changes. "You good man," he says. "You my friend."

Hallucinating in the late afternoon haze we found

and lost again our incoming tracks with negative help from delirious George. We had drunk none of the hot beer and Firth shared my distress signals of dehydration. In the rear-vision mirror our sprawling passengers merge with the gear in an oily mess, black and peppered red ochre. Believing the sump to be holed we stop. Leaning back to rescue an overnight bag it seems nailed to the floor. On a change of clothes in the unzipped bag is an oily black foot. A four litre container oozing engine oil tells all — our thirsty friends had taken a swig and tossed it aside in disgust. Later George proposed skin brothership. Have I earned it?

Jabiru or
Black-necked stork
(Zenorhynchus asiaticus)
also called the policeman bird.
Heron group; unlike herons
storks have no call. The
Jabiru, Australia's only
stork, produces a low pitched
boom, and clattering sounds
made by shaking its bill.
The Jabiru is also found
in New Guinea and in
Southern Asia.
It stands up to 1.2 metres,
is 1.5 metres in length
and has a wing span of
more than 2 metres.
The eye of the male is dark and
that of the female yellow.

Flooded depressions are carpeted with small yellow lilies and thousands of grass and whistle duck flock around the lone, immaculate Jabiru.

Late season thunder storms over the catchments have swollen the rivers. Jim Jim Creek appears no deeper than others crossed this afternoon but close to the far bank the Land Rover wallows deep in a channel. Water, red with sand, is seat-deep in the cabin. Miraculously the motor is still turning as reverse is engaged and doggedly propels the heavy vehicle back two hundred metres to drier sand, the exhaust spluttering like a boat.

A heavily built man with a swag of bedding and a bicycle across his shoulders wades the creek clutching a briefcase and a big gun. His unshaven features under a pith helmet transport me back to the thirties — Clark Gable in some tropical classic. But this is Dave Lindner, whose personal vendetta against uranium mining and buffalo is legend. For the past century buffalo have been shot from horseback, from vehicles and now from helicopters but continue to multiply and damage the ecology.

But Dave is cleaning up his area around Jim Jim on foot, single-handed. That's why he carries a gun. At home he keeps a buffalo, a pet — young but strong enough to toss you off your feet. Playful with widely splayed horns it likes to nuzzle between your thighs then jerk its head up — painful fun. Buffaloes preoccupy Dave. He identifies with them. It is not uncommon for hunter and hunted to become one. This oneness occurs between torero and bull in the Spanish arena. And can one resist

Horns of the Hunter's Dilemma . 1984

a quote from Oscar Wilde's Ballad of Reading Gaol:

Yet each man kills the thing he loves,
By each let this be heard,
Some do it with a bitter look,
Some with a flattering word.
The coward does it with a kiss,
The brave man with a sword!

Public attitude towards the buffalo is ambivalent. Some believe this feral beast to be indigenous, a natural tourist attraction which should be protected. Others, appalled by the mass slaughter, turn their head away. In an effort to eradicate brucellosis and tuberculosis among the nation's cattle herds it is planned to kill upwards of 200,000 wild buffalo by 1992. Some are being channelled through domestic farms for live export and slaughtering for human consumption and pet food. Within seven years the only live buffalo will be fenced in or in herds farmed by Aborigines for their beef consumption.

Seven years ago Dave Lindner raised the serious question of buffalo damage to the Kakadu's natural irrigation system. Wading between waterholes buffalo created channels to release fresh water into the tidal rivers. At king tides the waterholes filled with

saltwater. Already some areas of freshwater, highly fertile swamp had returned to the arid clay flat it had been before natural reclamation.

From his boat on Yellow Waters he drew my attention to the clear water of Jim Jim Creek meeting and merging with the opaque yellow of the South Alligator river. In April 1983 as he photographed this rewarding evidence of the success of his personal campaign against buffalo, which had previously polluted the creek and its waterholes near Jim Jim, his ambivalence toward this beast seemed to be resolved.

Dave lives at Patonga, one time shooting lodge

for weatlhy sportsmen. Now it is owned by Aborigines. There is a school for black, half-caste and white children — the teachers are white. The children's paintings are enchanting. Beside the ranch-style house is a scatter of buffalo skulls and by the entrance on the lawn rests the severed head of a grizzly bull, scarred in countless challenges to his harem during a long life.

"Grab some corn flakes," Dave offers from the open kitchen but I am more taken by the packet of 'Weet-bix' in a glass case which is food and shelter for a pair of marsupial mice.

Under leaves and bark
in another case
two

Asian
water buffalo.
Bubalus bubalis

death adders sleep. To my, "Dangerous company," he replies, "I like snakes." Shutters open to allow soft light from under the wide eaves into the timber and bamboo interior. The contents are simple and personal: Five saddles on a rail, beds with mosquito nets furled, buffalo horns under a table and on a cabinet with bark paintings, carvings of crocodiles, a floral plaque, a police association shield — the possessions of a loner. He talks of buffalo splattering rock art galleries and using them as rubbing stations. He is well informed on

archeological sites in the area. In 1972 he made important finds at Nauwalabila in Deaf Adder Gorge. The site was investigated in 1981 by Rhys Jones who tested crayons of ochre found there though not natural to the area. Ochres are known to have been traded over considerable distances and these crayons with ground and grooved edges have been dated to more than 25,000 years b.p. Ochre has no use other than as a decorative medium so life in that pre-historic time was not entirely a mind-numbing struggle for survival. On the eastern side of the continent at Lake Mungo the cremated remains of a female were found to belong to a similar period; the bones had been smashed and placed near the funerary pyre, a rite still practised when Europeans arrived. At another site the body of a lone male, not cremated but thickly coated with ochre, seems to complete the evidence that a woman was not simply chattel to be tossed in with her master as happened to Tutenkamen's wives.

The enlightening days in Dave's company came to an end when he drove me back along the Jim Jim highway — as far as the swollen creeks would allow. These we waded balancing heavy gear on our heads, a weight which proved to be useful ballast in the chest-deep, powerful current of Jim Jim — a fateful creek for wild-life film maker Malcolm Douglas. Water was swirling inside the cabin of his Land cruiser which had nosed into the channel I had managed to reverse out of a few days back.

Malcolm's equipment was saturated. Smiling bitterly he opened camera cases and exposed many lenses to dry on a towel. "Waste of time," the big man said. "they will have to be properly cleaned in a laboratory in Sydney." And of the truck he estimated $3000 mechanical damage. The end of a journey which was to have taken him by boat along the South Alligator river to Van Diemen Gulf then the north coast and islands in the Arafura Sea as far as the Gulf of Carpentaria. He had wanted particularly to film crocodiles.

Pointing to Dave I said, "Here's the man to fill you in about crocodiles. He captured Sweetheart, the great Museum showpiece". Malcolm was impressed but Dave was self-effacing as he told of his attempt to move the 5·1 metre male estuarine from Finniss river to a more suitable waterhole. As Dave winched it from the river, headfirst with great jaws firmly tied, Sweetheart drowned. Sadly he explained it should have been hauled by the tail to avoid intake of water to the lungs. Taking its affectionate dubbing from Sweets Look-out Sweetheart had been thought to be female.

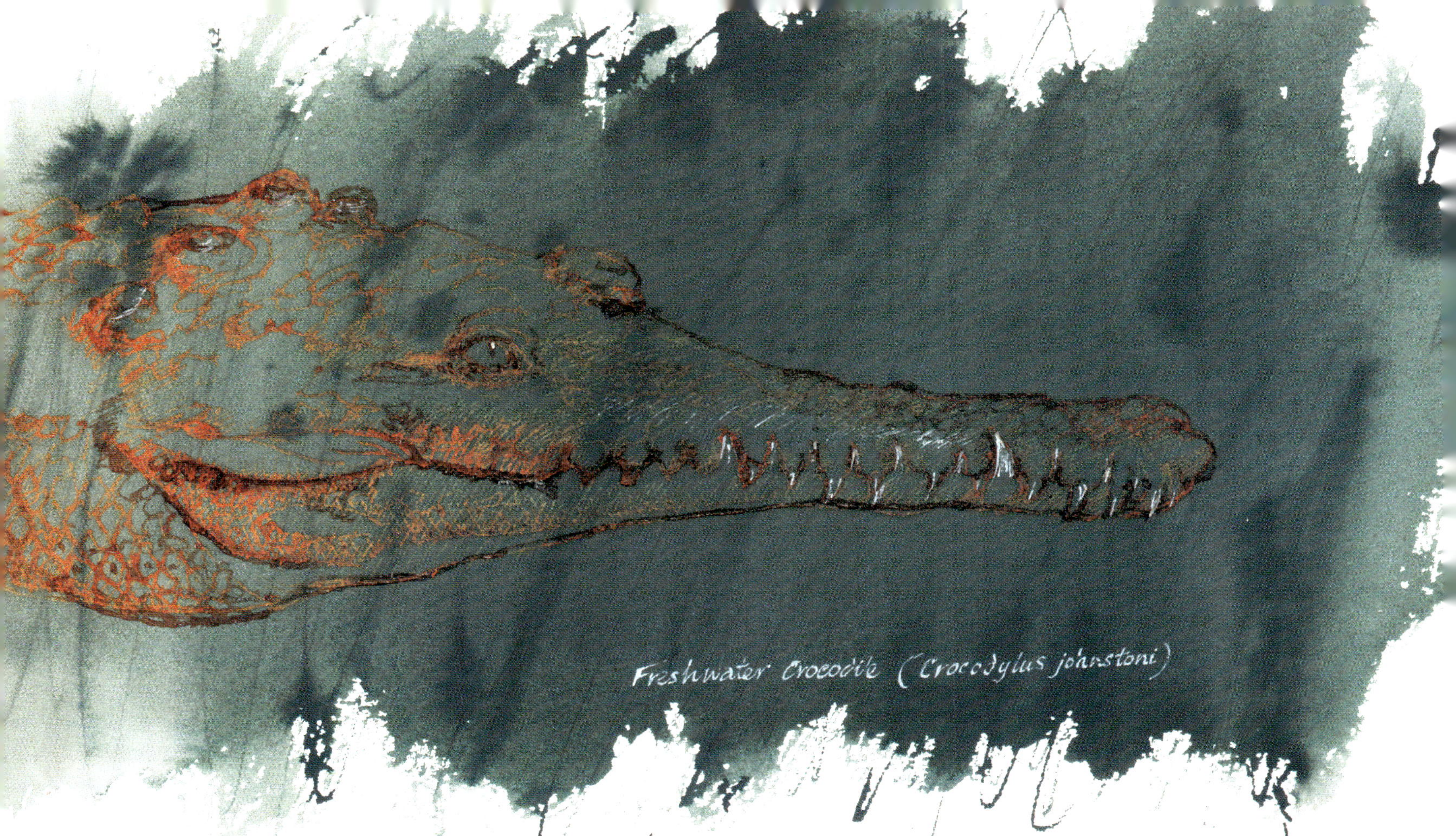

Freshwater Crocodile (Crocodylus johnstoni)

Saltwater Crocodile (Crocodylus porosus)

Thought to have been on earth 180 million years crocodiles have survived substantially unchanged. They evolved from a prehistoric species of reptile related to alligators.

Two species are found in Arnhem Land, the freshwater and the saltwater or estuarine. While 'freshies' as they are called locally, are indigenous to Australia 'salties' occur in India and South East Asia down through the Indo-Malaysia Archipelago to Papua New Guinea and our tropical North. 'Freshies' present no threat to man but 'salties' will attack without provocation. Though the speed of attack (they can out-sprint man) makes identification difficult it could prove useful to know that the killer, the saltwater crocodile, has a broader and shorter snout. The finer beak-like snout of the freshwater crocodile makes it the more attractive of the two. Also, in line across the neck behind the flat of the head are four large scales.

The eye of the killer is built like a helmet with a vizor. Both eyes and nostrils are protected by flaps which close automatically when submerged. Strategically positioned on top of the head these organs allow the crocodile to immerse the great mass of its body and achieve perfect camouflage yet observe and breathe.

As with many nocturnal animals the eye of the crocodile has evolved a highly reflective tapetum which gives it the advantage of every twinkle of starlight. It works in much the same way as do cats' eyes set in a highway. This ingenious device evolved for the crocodile long before man's invention of the flashlight. Given all its natural camouflage, a glitter of red reflecting a spot of light and the crocodile's cover is blown.

Propelled by webbed rear feet and a muscular tail flattened like a paddle and swished from side to side both species are powerful swimmers. Both feed on fish and aquatic animals but the saltwater crocodile preys on larger animals — anything from dog to buffalo.

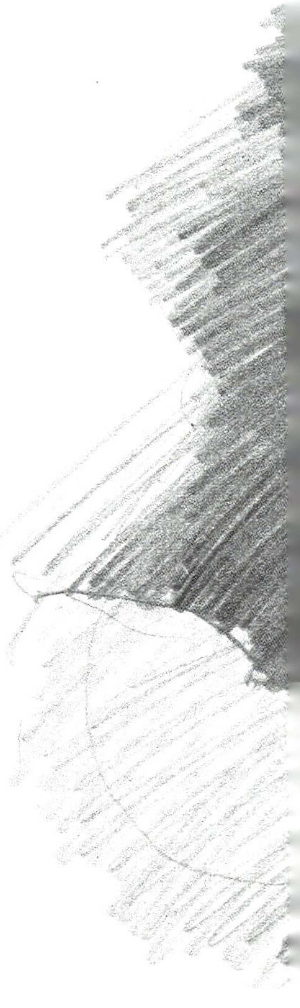

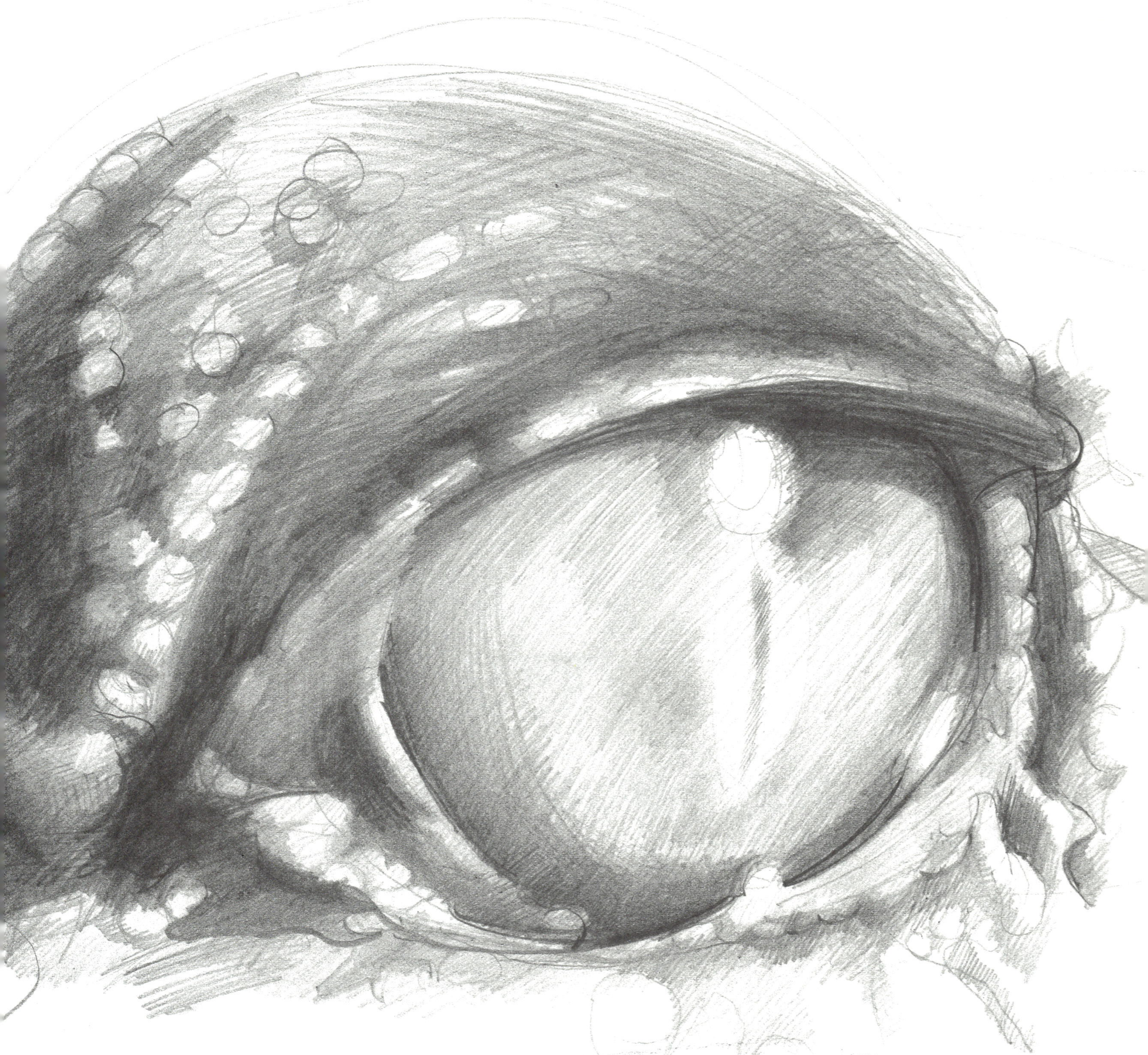

Crocodiles play an important role in maintaining the natural balance in nature. As carnivores they help regulate the abundance of wild life and thus conserve the unique character of the floating landscape they inhabit.

Their flesh and eggs are prime food for Aboriginals who find the entrails useful too as medicine. The teeth are kept as charms. Taking only what they needed for food during 40,000 years of co-existence Aboriginals did not disturb the ecology.

In just 150 years Europeans massacred crocodiles in such numbers that survival of the species became critical. Hunting at night from boats shooters found the ruby-red eyes reflected in spotlight an easy target. A single ·303 bullet at close range can destroy the brain. A harpoon was thrust into the body which was quickly lashed to the boat. The belly skin alone was prized, the value estimated per inch across the girth. As the saltwater of the species became scarce rising prices of its leather created a demand for the smaller and lower quality skin of the freshwater.

Monoprint — after Ryko photos in the National Archives F.H.

facial feathers white
with buff and black tips —
rufous around eyes —
also known as
chestnut-faced owl
Masked owl
Cave owl or Maw-faced owl
(Tyto novaehollandiae)
Wing and back feathers buff —
upper parts dark grey and brown
Underparts white or buff —
black spots on breast
and flank
Feathered to feet — short and
bristly on toes

Though the glaring heat of day departs with the sun the ash-grey sand underfoot is warm. Nevertheless we drag another ant-eaten log onto the fire and kick it back to life. It brightens the spirits and the smoke screens us from insects. Beyond our circle of flickering shadows the night is alive with creatures foraging for the broadcast scraps of our evening meal — scratching and chittering.

Our ears tune to a variety of calls, mostly owls. A persistent wook-wook leading to a chorus of barking then isolated growls like a pack of dogs is in fact produced by Barking Owls. At the other end of the scale this owl is capable of a loud screech, pitched high, earning it the dubbing of Screaming Woman. Softer is the mournful woo-hoo of the Rufous Owl. A rasping screech from behind a rocky outcrop draws us to close inspection. In a crevice, by torch-light a Masked Owl crouches, moving its head from side to side then in a circle. Wings spread it hisses and snaps at us.

Barking Owl — Winking owl or Screaming Woman (Ninox connivens)

Rufous Owl (Ninox rufa)

Impressions are so fleeting: a bird lights on a branch and flies on, a goanna pauses to check the camp kitchen, shadows change place, the escarpment flares and blackens. Bats we hear rather than see as small mammals forage among fallen leaves. The clear sapphire sky is now indigo, a massive body covered with jet. Through the masquito net screw palms spin like catherine wheels. The stars spin above the encircling horizon and giddily I know that we live not in this world but on it, pressed to its outer edge — it would be easy to drop out into the universe. Back in the Dreaming men, women and animals fleeing from disaster on earth leapt to the sky for safety. They lost their earthly disguise in the glitter of stars; each is a home for their spirits. The spirit of a dead person is transported on a shooting star. Aborigines believe the sun to be woman, constantly wandering, broadcasting light and warmth, cohabiting with her moon man briefly during eclipse.'

As the eye adjusts to the bat-black of night there is plenty of light and colour is subtle — a different world of creatures which see only at night. Monet denied black its right to be called a colour. He said it didnot exist in nature but that did not prevent his black moods. Matisse, on the other hand, claimed black as a positive colour of light.

Before dawn some creature stalks my plastic ground-sheet with hesitant though heavy tread. To my ear on the ground it sounds more like a crocodile than a buffalo. Cold sweat clams the hands but spotted in torchlight it is only a tiny marsupial mouse.

Over bacon and eggs at breakfast squatting around the camp fire I laughed with George Chaloupka about my nocturnal visitor. Nipper, spooked by the night as most Aborigines are, said, "Not like dat pella" "That plastic?" I ask, "Why?" "Him talk too much." Here again each object has a spirit and abilities such as those normally attributed to humans

Nipper refused breakfast claiming to have had a couple of beers. "A chop in every can," he declared.

The Artists' camp — Blue Tongue Dreaming — with Clifton Pugh

Termite track over Rock Art — near Blue Tongue

Thylacine and cub after thousands of years under a na protective coating of silica. (From a rock pain on the escarpmen

Mad dogs and painters at noon — the crackling yellow grass, head high, encloses oven heat. Clif is working in a sliver of shade from a small outlying rock. Offering a mug of warm barleywater I comment on one of many images on the rock face, an animal with apparent wattles: "Hadn't thought of goats up here." "And striped, that has to be a thylacine, look at the 'straight tail'." The wattles we decide are his supper. Archeologists say the thylacine has not prowled Arnhem Land for six thousand years. Perhaps an acid medium etched the painted line into the sandstone to preserve the image against such a time span. In silence we ponder what had the ancient in mind — symbol or simple sketch?

Two metres long from nose to tail this wolf-like marsupial's Latin name, Thylacinus cynocephalus, spells 'pouched dog with a wolf's head'. Though long extinct on the mainland it was plentiful in Tasmania till the turn of the century when it was shot out by bounty hunters. Though there have been reports of recent sightings the last known thylacine died in captivity in 1933. More striped than the Bengal tiger it is commonly known as the Tasmanian tiger.

Red-cheeked
Dunnart
(Sminthopsis virginiae
nitela)
found in top end of N.T., Kimberleys &
the east coast of Cape York Penin.

A loner but
extremely social in
the wet, its breeding season.
The female builds a shallow
circular nest of dry
leaves and grass just
before her six or more
young are born.

Average length: 100 mm
tail: 110 mm.

Short fur, white tipped
dark grey above,
rufous yellow below.

Sugar Glider (Petaurus breviceps ariel). Marsupial.
Average head-body length: 170 mm. Tail: 190 m.m.
Blue to brown grey above with dorsal stripe black, tail black, at times tipped white; creamy pale-grey below.
Feeds on gum of acacias and eucalypts, also invertebrates.
Nests in leaf lined hollows in trees and rocks and lives in small social groups. The female carries her two young in the pouch for about 70 days.
Sugar gliders scream when fighting,
gurgle and chatter when disturbed
and their yapping is shrill
when prey to cats
or owls.

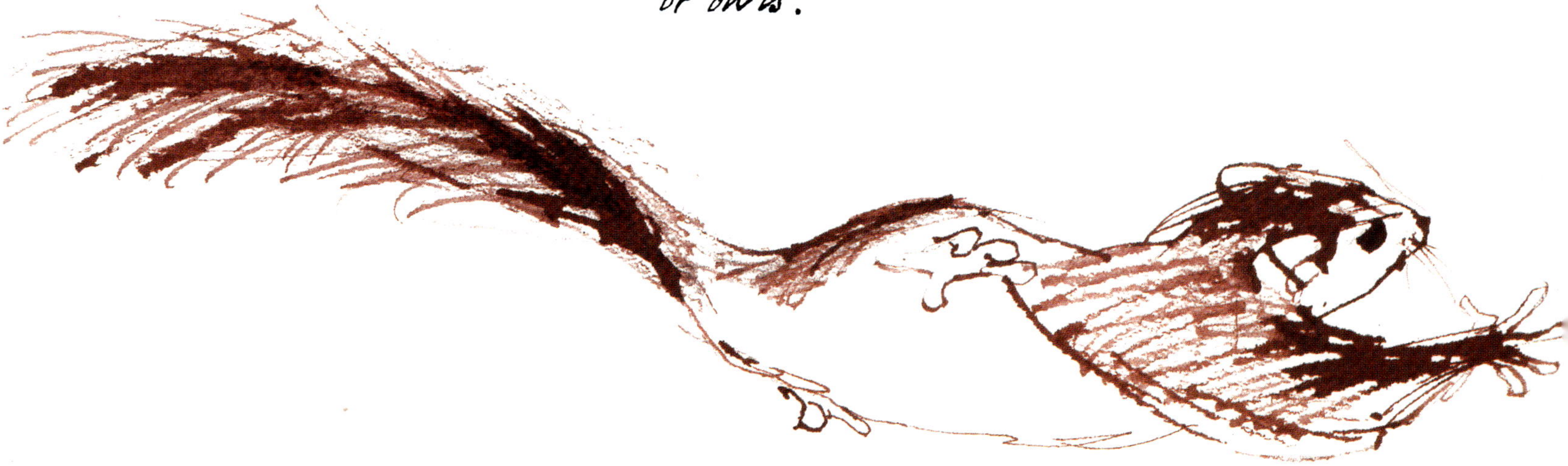

Pushing off with hindlegs the sugar glider spreads membranes which extend from its feet. Steering by curving the membranes it can glide fifty and more metres. Swinging its hindlegs forward it makes a four point landing on the bark of a tree.

Piles of stones I had thought to be cairns others had taken for headstones and named this Graveside Gorge, but George Chaloupka assures me these are simply hunting markers. Hunters wait at these markers of known wallaby tracks to spear game flushed out by the fired scrub.

The gorge is high in the escarpment and a bitter wind drives through it. Nipper tells us this cleavage in the towering escarpment was made by an ancestor named Bilk bilk who, in the form of a big bird (a galah, 'cacatua roseicapilla'), flew through the rock.

Tranquil and refreshing after the four and a half hour haul from Jim Jim, Bilk bilk mi creek cascades through the gorge and forms a pool of Olympic proportions at our campsite. The scorched sand which had caused us to uproot trees while winching the heavily laden Rover and trailer out of deep drifts now provides a cool white beach.

In the shade of an Anbanadja* tree. Nipper explains its other useful quality. The lazy fisherman crushes the bark and leaves of this tree with a stone and introduces their juices to the creek water — the fish are stunned, "make him drunk" says Nipper, so they float on the surface and are easily taken.

* Owenia Vernicosa

The Bilkbilkmi track

Among many groups in central and western Arnhem Land Luma Luma, the great Dreaming Whale is credited with the ancient revelation of ritual signs. In bark paintings the whale is represented not in natural form but by the designs he created: the rainbow or clouds and thunder as abstracted in this detail of a painting from Yirrkala.

Goulburn Islands -

The saga of the beach-washed whale. A revelation of Aboriginal spiritual values contaminated by European materialism in negotiations for possession of the whale's skeleton. Is it substance or spirit, scientific specimen or revered ancestor? The contemporary spiritual significance of whales is a reverance predated by Aboriginal mythology and beliefs.

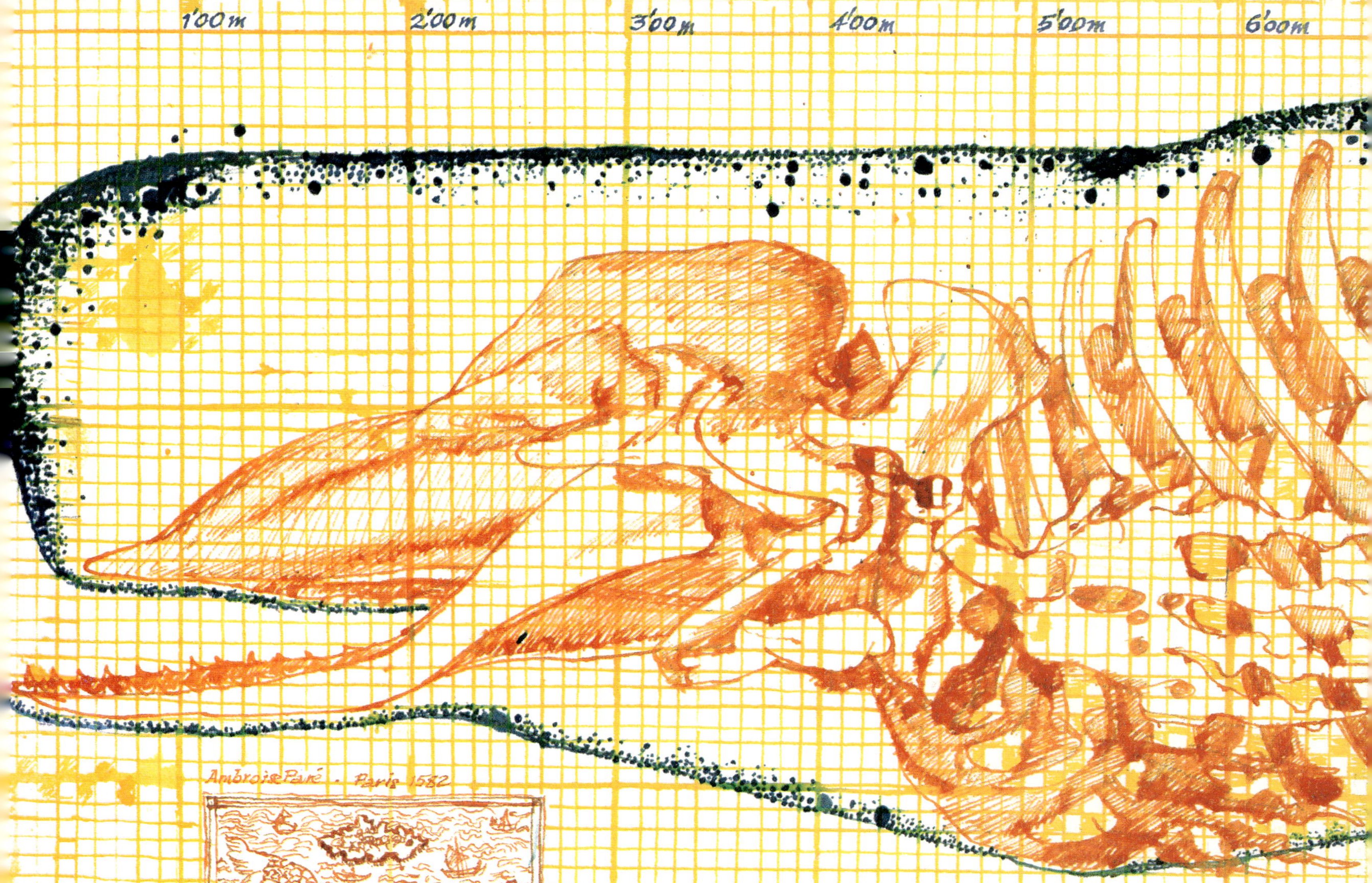

Ambroise Paré · Paris 1582

"Genius in the Sperm Whale? Has the Sperm Whale ever written a book, spoken a speech? No, his great genius is declared in doing nothing particular to prove it. It is moreover declared in his pyramidical silence. And this reminds me that had the great Sperm Whale been known to the young Orient World, he would have been deified by their child-magician thoughts.... If hereafter any highly cultured, poetical nation shall lure back to their birthright, the merry May-day gods of old; and livingly enthrone them again in the now egotistical sky; in the now unhaunted hill; then be sure, exalted to Jove's high seat, the great Sperm Whale shall lord it...." so wrote Herman Melville in Moby Dick.

Cetaceans (whale order of mammals) have fascinated mankind since the beginning of art. Their awesome proportions,

from Westminster Abbey
12th C. A.D.

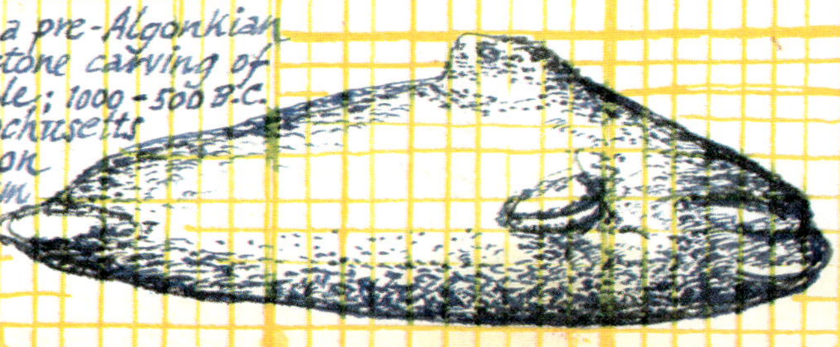

from a pre-Algonkian soapstone carving of a whale; 1000-500 B.C. Massachusetts Bronson Museum

8'00m 9'00m 10'00m 11'00m 1200 1300m 14

from a stele, Carthage, 200 B.C. The dolphin was sacred, a symbol of the Carthaginians' supreme deity, the goddess Tanit.

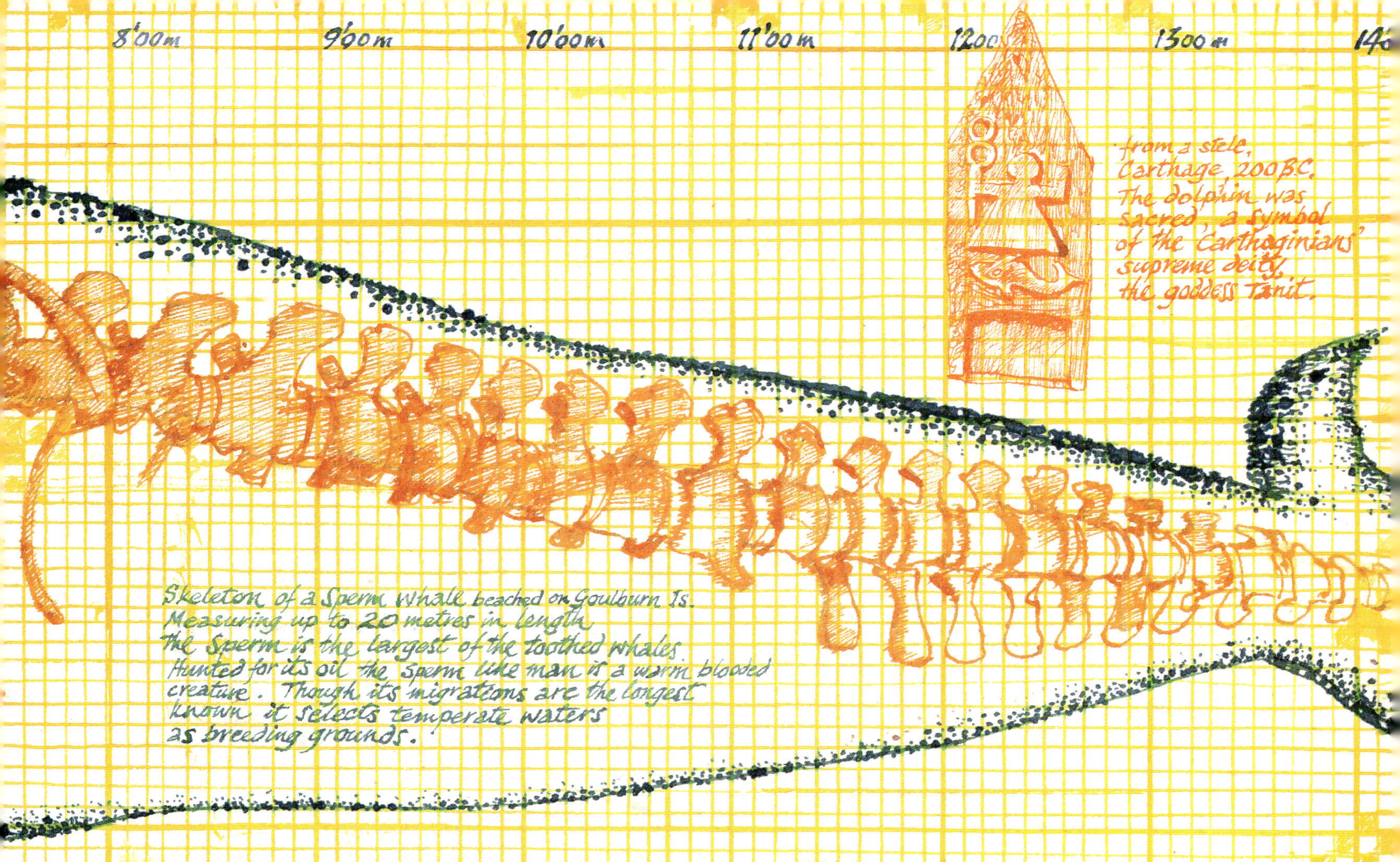

Skeleton of a Sperm Whale beached on Goulburn Is. Measuring up to 20 metres in length the Sperm is the largest of the toothed whales. Hunted for its oil the Sperm like man is a warm blooded creature. Though its migrations are the longest known it selects temperate waters as breeding grounds.

their intriguing ability to think and play, always a mystery, have inspired poets from the antiquity of Plutarch to the present day. In "Whales Weep Not!" D.H. Lawrence expressed:

> "They say the sea is cold, but the sea contains
> the hottest blood of all, and the wildest, the most urgent.
> All the whales in the wider deeps, hot they are, as they urge
> on and on, and dive beneath the icebergs."

Artists have made images of Jonah and the Whale, most popular of biblical tales, in a thousand and more varied ways. Having no direct experience with whales artists of antiquity based their monstrous depictions on the colourful tales of sailors returning from voyages in uncharted oceans. Giotto's fresco in the Arena Chapel of Padua shows Jonah being swallowed by a large fish rather than a gigantic mammal.

The earliest known images of whales are the mesolithic carvings in rocks on Norwegian shores; ca 5000 B.C.

Jonah and the Whale
fresco by Giotto, 1305 A.D.
Padua, Italy.

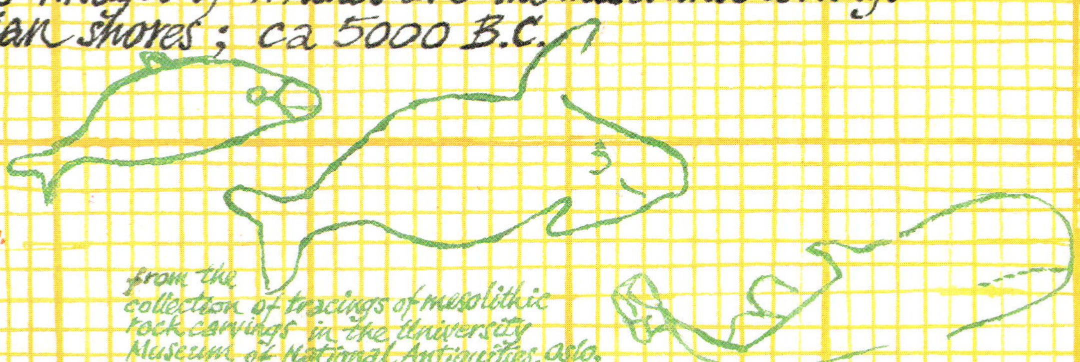

from the collection of tracings of mesolithic rock carvings in the University Museum of National Antiquities, Oslo.

More recently, in the 1930s, canvases by Vassily Kandinsky contained stylised images of whales.

Skeletal forms fascinated artists long before Leonardo da Vinci; and in our own times the skull of a great mammal dominated Julian Huxley's garden in London. Even with a patina of industrial fall-out the mammoth form created such a deep impression on his friend Henry Moore that Huxley gave it to him. Moore had his sculptor assistants, many of whom have been Australians, clean it and later completed a series of lithographs based on this monumental skull.

For perhaps six times the estimated 7000 years of the mesolithic rock carvings in Norway the whale has played an important totemic role among Aboriginal people in North and East Arnhem Land and Cape York Peninsula. Here and on the islands offshore cloud patterns, particularly the black ones which thunder and flash, are associated with the great whale ancestor. In the beginning the creator whale formed the clouds by spraying the sky with mist and revealed the ritual signs for them – a pattern of triangles used in ceremony to this day among clans such as the Waramiri.

The Aboriginal's oneness with his surroundings, his unambitious life style, his art and nature constantly reflecting one another, recalls Melville's line about the whale: "…. his great genius is declared in doing nothing particular to prove it."

The great Ancestor Whale spouted symbolic rainbows to glow in the big black clouds of the threatening monsoon but was fatally trapped in the shallows on the receding tide near Milingimbi. Its death established the great Dreaming Site at Gurrumiya where seasonally whales beach themselves and, according to the Girrkirr, nowhere else. But there are other Whale Dreaming sites; even close to the city of Darwin, on a reef at Southport. And in 1980 a fourteen metre Sperm whale beached on Goulburn Island to create another sacred site for the Aboriginal community and a bizarre situation for the white authorities in Darwin.

TELECOM AUSTRALIA

TRY 818739

Office Date Stamp

2.

TELEGRAM

TX 42. C N C46397/74-L

VM8EO WARRUWI OPR DARWIN NT 50/49 9.18AM

TELEPHONED
TO
TIME 1.06 p
INTLS
POSTBOX

58
~~TF818379~~
DIRECTOR JACK HINTON
MUSEUM
DARWIN NT
x Box 4646

AWAITING YOUR REPRESENTATIVE OR YOURSELF TO TALK AT GOULBURN ISLAND RE WHALE SKELETON MOVEMENT TO DARWIN MUSEUM THIS IS THE DECISION AS WE HAVE CHANGED IT WE NEED BARGE BEFORE WET SEASON STARTS TRY TO GET HERE TODAY

...BURRUMARRA MBE CHAIRMAN TRIBAL COUNCIL

CPD 11.45AMSF

First sighted on November the 18th the whale was stranded in the middle of a kilometre and a half wide reef. King tides had later carried it inshore and wedged it tail first in the mangroves. Interested in collecting a complete whale skeleton for the Museum of Arts and Sciences the Director had taxidermist Ian Archibald flown to Goulburn Island on the 24th November to assess the practicability of

macerating the bones on the spot for shipment to Darwin.
An escort of black and white officials including the President of the Warruwi Community, the Town Clerk and an Aboriginal Community Advisor took Ian on his initial visit to the whale. Resting on its reef damaged right side this male sperm whale's upper side was intact and Archibald estimated about three weeks of tedious work separating the skeleton from its already pungent carcass. He recovered two teeth from the broken right jaw and was contemplating the removal and labelling of all teeth to avoid loss and facilitate later reconstruction when his party was challenged by an aggressive group of six blacks. Bearing a cloth patterned with geometric sacred symbols and armed with three shovel-nosed spears complete with womera the leader, John Gurruwiwi, an elder from Elcho Island, threatened death to the uninitiated who dared look upon his totem whale; it was human, a symbol of his people's Mother-Father Dreaming. He claimed one million dollars as the value of just one bone and the entire carcass would be flown back to Elcho Island.
The Goulburn Islanders felt that fate had beached the whale on their territory and their President said he would be proud to have the skeleton housed in the new Darwin Museum.
Back in Darwin the Museum plans for the skeleton were thwarted even further by proposals before Parliament in a new Northern Territory Fisheries Act and another drafted by National Parks and Wild Life to prohibit the collection and use of beach washed whales.

From Goulburn Island the Town Clerk reported yet another complication involving the whale's sperm oil: restrictions may be placed on the manner of processing it and its sale for white man's profit; also on how many whites could come to the island for the recovery operation.

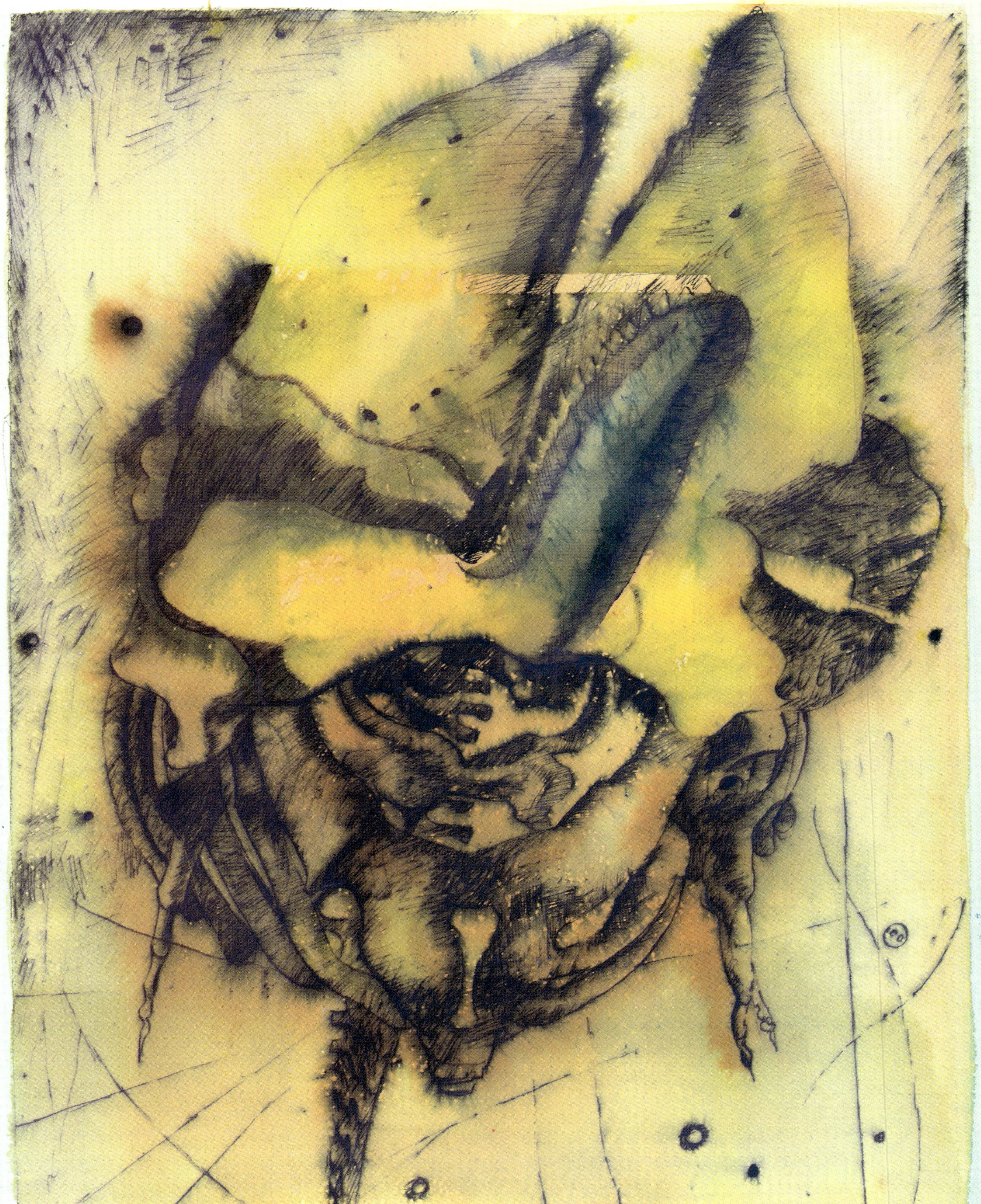

At the request of the Goulburn and Elcho Islanders Ian Archibald, representing the Museum, returned for further discussions about the final resting place of the beached whale. He was accompanied by an aborigine from Milingimbi, a field officer of the Northern Land Council, whose knowledge of the local dialect proved useful in subsequent proceedings.

David Burramarra, inseparable from his M.B.E., chaired a succession of meetings, the first at three in the afternoon of December 16th. Among those present were the chairman of the Elcho Island Wangurri clan and adviser to the Warruwi Community, George Daymbu and Galbu clan members John Lawurra and Mathaman, both children of the Whale. Archibald and a Uniting Church adviser to the Warruwi were the only whites at the meeting.

A typed sheet was tabled itemising thirteen points for discussion. It was stated that Elcho Islanders were shocked and felt shame and were angry when they heard about the fate of the whale and, initially, had refused to allow its skeleton to go to Darwin. Two senators, Willy M.B.E. and Munyu, had proposed to Galiwinku that the law be changed; then with the consent of John Lawurra, child of the Whale, it was agreed that the skeleton could be moved and housed in the Darwin museum.

But ... before this precious animal of the Arafura Sea could be moved certain rites had to be performed; these included singing, dancing and feasting in accordance with their sacred beliefs. Money was needed for one hundred people to fly to Goulburn Island from Galiwinku, Milingimbi and Yirrkala for the ceremony and their accommodation, needs from the store, such as food and drink, must be met. It was proposed that the Chief Minister be approached to approve these funds, which, it was suggested, could be raised jointly by his Department, the Northern Territory Museum, the Northern Land Council, the Aboriginal Cultural Foundation and the Arnhem Land Fund.

1. WHALE ON A BEACH OF GOULBURN ISLAND.

2. STORY FROM GOULBURN ISLAND TO ELCHO ISLAND ABOUT THE WHALE.

3. WE SAID NO,SKELETON SHOULD NOT GO TO DARWIN MUSEUM .

4. TWO SENATORS OF GALIWINKU ASKED GALIWINKU TO CHANGE THAT LAW SO THAT THE SKELETON COULD GO TO DARWIN MUSEUM. THE NAMES OF THE TWO MEN ARE WILLY M.B.E.&MUNYU.

5. BARGE SHOULD COME FROM DARWIN TO GOULBURN ISLAND TO LOAD SKELETON FOR DARWIN MUSEUM.

6. MONEY FOR THE SKELETON OF THE CEREMONIAL ANIMAL A PRESCIOUS ANIMAL IN THE ARAFURA SEA MONEY SHOULD BE TO PAY AND SATISFY ABORINGINAL BELEIFS AND TRADITIONAL FRAME OF LAW THIS IS IN THE SEA EXACTLY AS MINERAL ON THE LAND AND THIS IS THE CEREMONAL CARE OF THE ANCESSORS.

7. MONEY OF THIS SKELETON MOVEMENT TO DARWIN MONEY SHOULD BECOMING FROM ABORIGINAL CULTURAL FOUNDATION. I ASK CULTURAL FOUNDATION FOR ADVICE AND SUPPORT ,FOR THE BARGE AND FOR THE PEOPLE TRAVELLING ARRAINGMENT FROM GALIWINKU MILINGIMBIE YIRRAKALA TO GOULBURN ISLAND FOR THE CEREMONY, WE NEED THIS SUPPORT TO ENABLE PEOPLE TO TRAVELL TO GOULBURN ISLAND .

8. BARGE HAS TO BE IN GOULBURN ISLAND BEFORE THE WET SEASON STARTS. WE PICK GOULBURN ISLAND PEOPLE TO BE IN THE CEREMONY SINGING AND DANCING WITH YIRRAKALA AND GALIWINKU AT THE SAME TIME.

9. ALSO WE ASK GOULBURN ISLAND COUNCIL TO GUARD ON THIS BUSINESS. WE NEED TWO BIG TRUCKS TO CARRY SKELETON TO THE BARGE. GOULBURN ISLAND COMMUNITY DEV. CENTRE TO BE THERE ALSO.

10. IF MONEY SHORT IN CULTURAL FOUNDATION THE DARWIN NORTHERN LAND COUNCIL OR THE MUSEUM IN DARWIN . THESE THREE DEPARTMENTS SHOULD TIE UP IN BUNDLE AND LISTEN FOR THE WISHES OF THE ABORIGINAL PEOPLE THAT THEY ARE ASKING FOR MONEY. THESE THREE DEPARTMENTS WORK THROUGH WELFARE OF ABORIGINAL PEOPLE AND SATISFY THEIR DESIRES.

11. IF THESE THREE DEPARTMENTS CAN NOT SATISFY THEN ARNHEMLAND FUNDSSHOULD PROVIDE MONEY FOR THIS MOVEMENTSHIP.

12. WE RECOMMEND BARGE VISIT MIDDLE OF CHRISTMAS WEEK.

13. GOULBURN ISLAND PEOPLE MUST HAVE A SAY IN THE WORD OF THIS CEREMONY OF WHALE SKELETON ACCORDING TO THAT CREATION THE BEGINING OF NORTH AUSTRALIA THINGS IN THE SEA AND THINGS ON THE LAND ARE ANIMAL OR MINERAL AND ABORIGINAL PEOPLE HAVE RELATIONSHIP AND KINSHIP. THIS IS THE SAME WAY OF LIFE AND DISCUSS MATTER LIKE LAND RIGHTS ACT.

"The Chairman explained how Emu, Kangaroo and Turkey were on the land and that in the Sea the Whale was the highest and the dolphin was the lowest in importance in tribal tradition. He spoke on public and sacred dances and explained how for 5,000 years Aboriginal Culture, law and language had been practised here....

"The Chairman stated that the whale's skin should go to Elcho Island ... but I suggested that after three weeks in the sun it would be too rotten for this.

"It was suggested after much discussion that the royalty be raised from $12,000 to $1,200,000 as all must have a share and

▲ from a painted wood carving of a whale or dugong. Yirrkalla

there was a big population of traditional people, and I stated that this was impractical as it was a quarter of the cost of the new Museum and there were too many other items of greater importance for which we could use that amount of money."

The third meeting was called more formally at Transit House starting at 8 p.m. and finishing at midnight.

"The Chairman started by showing a photo of the Chief Minister, Mr. P. Everingham, the Administrator of the Northern Territory, Mr. John England, the Leader of the Opposition, Mr. John Isaacs, the Member for Arnhem, Mr. Bob Collins and the coat of arms for the Northern Territory plus several other photos of groups of people all on a background of tribal motifs as on the sign leading to the 'whale beach.'

In his report to the Museum Ian Archibald recorded that "The Chairman wanted the barge next week and I stated that this was not feasible as the preparation of the skeleton would not be ready. (At this stage I hadn't seen the whale which had now been decomposing for three weeks on the beach and was a much easier job than before.)

"The Chairman then asked if we had any medicine in Darwin that we could put on the body of the whale to take away the smell. I replied no, and he asked if Perth would have some and I again replied no, and added not Perth or anywhere in the world was there a medicine that can stop approximately forty tonnes of putrefying meat smelling in tropical conditions.

"The Chairman then stated that the teeth were not part of the skeleton and mentioned that whale teeth were the only way of getting into Fiji, but he did not elaborate on that. I explained that to the Museum the skeleton was not complete without teeth." (Research revealed that a Fijian chieftain wears a whale's tooth pendant.)

Fourteen kilometres from the Warruwi settlement at the last turn off to the mangrove entangled whale site the elders had erected a sign of geometrical shapes, a pattern of symbolic triangles which warned the uninitiated to keep clear of this sacred area. On his second inspection Archibald found that the "animal had broken down to a remarkable extent in the last two weeks and many ribs and vertebrae have been collected by John Lawurra and placed above the high water mark on the shore or in the mangrove trees on the tidal flat. John has also collected and cleaned thirty one teeth (plus two I had collected earlier) which were at his home along with five of the discs on the backbone."

The next meeting to discuss "Royalty regarding Whale skeleton" began at 6p.m. Archibald continues his report:

"The Chairman stated that the Royalty or compensation money should be to the satisfaction and happiness of traditional owners because the whale was a very ceremonial animal to do with the creator in the aboriginal mind.

"The Chairman suggested that because the whale was thirty feet long* we would be talking of 10 or 12 number money. I thought this was fair (thinking of $300 to $360) but asked for clarification and was told the number of 1000, making $10,000 – $12,000.... I suggested that the cost of the royalty was too high and way above what the Museum was able or willing to pay, especially combined with the cost of the dances etc., and was told that the other sources mentioned could help out.

"I pointed out that there was another problem with the display of this sacred animal which was that it would be viewed by all — men, women and children and that we could not segregate or restrict the people visiting the Museum. I asked whether the Elders would like the sacred association regarding the whale played up or interpreted to the public when on display and they said no.

* Actual size of the whale was more than 40 feet

"Most of the night was taken up with matters relating to the royalty and during the course of the evening it was established the travel money, regarding song and dance, and the royalty money were separate matters. The Elders discussed whether this price was to be yearly or once and forever and I stated they should work on a once and forever price as the museum, if interested, would not pay yearly.

"Liwukang of the Warramirri clan stated that he thought $1,200,000 was too much and suggested that $90,000 would be better. He then counted up to 90 on his fingers and said that even that number at $1000 each was too much, but this was overruled.

"Stating that the whale was someone in the world the Elders moved a motion that the skeleton must be in the Law and they made the Law there and then that from 1980 and thereafter and forevermore . . . .

"This was agreed to by:

Burramarra M.B.E.	Warramirri
Liwukang	Warramirri
Lawurra	Galbu (Child of Whale)
Mathaman	Galbu (Child of Whale)
Rev. Terry Djiniyini (wasn't in attendance)	Galamola (Child of Whale)
George Daymbu (not at meeting either)	Wangurri
Gomumk (one woman) Lamirri - tribal name	Owner of the whale

and also Phillip, the Uniting Church Minister on Goulburn Island.

The Chairman stated that "This is the Law" and that there should be a picture of each of these people to go with the Law.

"Some discussion then on the breastbone of the whale which commanded a high price because it was God's shelter for the Missionary Jonah of Ninevah and it should receive extra special care.

"Discussion of badges came up and it was decided that there should be 2 badges issued to the Museum and 2 to the Northern Land Council. The badges bear the title Dhuldji Warramirri Council above a painted message in geometric design which, when read tells the story of the creation and the whale. These badges were to be worn whenever dealing with matters of the whale and also would enable the wearer to safely enter any area where another whale was beached or wherever a dance was being held regarding whales. (James Gurrwanngu felt this a great honour)."

"The next day, being Wednesday the 17th December, I made up a rough estimate of the costs so far talked about and submitted it to Burrumarra:

1	Already cost Museum $500 in fares and camping allowance..	
2	100 people to Goulburn (dance) at $150 return	$15,000
3	100 people to Darwin June dance at $300 return	$30,000
	plus stores and accommodation at say $10 - $15 per night	$15,000
4	Barge costs regarding transport of skeleton	$5,000
5	Casual labour 3 people $50 each and transport $50	$200 a day
6	Royalty Money	$90,000

"I told Burrumarra that the whale was too sacred and that the Museum and I felt the Government could not justify this kind of money. Burrumarra still felt that this request should be presented.... When asked what happens if the N.T. Govt. refuses he said they would go to the Federal Govt. and Aboriginal Affairs.

"This discussion.... went from Transit House to under a mango tree.... and included a session where Burrumarra tried to trade the whale's teeth for an order number to cover the cost of his return air ticket to Elcho Island...."

Late December monsoons blackened and lashed the Arafura Sea to pound the already broken remains of the great ancestor mammal on the shore of Goulburn Island. In Darwin the unresolved ceremonial and financial problems of the whale's disposal hovered over Christmas celebrations at the museum.

In an appeal to the Chief Minister's Aboriginal Liaison Unit acting Museum Director J.E.B. Syme wrote: "..... Initially, what started out as a simple exercise in acquiring a whale for the Museum at a reasonable estimated cost of say $6.000-$7000 has developed into a major sphere of argument/discussion with the cost escalating far beyond our resources. .... It would appear ... that the Aboriginal Councils seek further discussions. We are not competent to handle the situation and seek your assistance and advice ...."

On that given advice the Acting Museum Director wrote to David Burrumarra saying, "..... In recognising the religious importance of the whale, the Museum feels that it is unable to assume responsibility for it, and that it is more appropriate for custody and control to remain with its traditional Aboriginal owners."

Since mid November an overpowering smell had protected the whale's sanctity and made it impossible for the women to collect shellfish on the shores within some distance of the putrefying carcass. Perhaps it was the prevailing wind of late January carrying the pungent odour to the Warruwi settlement that caused the asking price to crash to $8000-$9000. In the February peak of the Wet the scattered remains of the skeleton were offered at $6000.

On the 27th March 1981 Museum Director Dr. Colin Jack-Hinton closed the file on the controversial whale with this letter to Mr. Burrumarra of Galiwinku, Elcho Island: "I have received your message through the mission concerning your desire to proceed with the ceremony for the whale at Goulburn Island and asking $ 6000 for, I presume, the sale of the whale and the ceremony.

The Museum understands the sacred significance of the whale to you, which is why, after it was indicated that you would require $ 1.3 million for it and even when you reduced this to $ 8/9000 the Museum decided not to touch the whale or remove it to Darwin. We feel that to do so would be an intrusion into your important ceremonial affairs. Our only interest in it was as a natural scientific specimen.

I am glad that you will still be going ahead with the ceremony, but we are unable to give you any financial assistance towards performing the ceremony. It might be advisable, if you are in need of funds, to approach another Aboriginal funding agency more able to support financially cultural religious activities of this nature."

The Northern Territory Government offered the traditional owners of the whale assistance in recovery of the whale's remains and in making arrangements for its housing at Elcho, Goulburn or both islands.

Long after the air had cleared of the whale business David Burrumarra gently chided Colin Jack-Hinton about the Museum's handling of the negotiations. Colin replied that the initial figure of $ 1.3 million was unrealistic, after all to the Museum it was only a whale, it was not "Blue Poles"! And anyway how was such a high figure arrived at? Quietly Burrumarra asked in reply, "What price would you put on your God?" "My God? Beyond price!"

Jonah and the Whale from an illumination in the Kennicott Bible in Hebrew, 1476. coll. Bodleian Library Oxford.

Gove Peninsula.

— A flight over the mangrove-entangled far-north coast, vibrant in colour and texture, returning to red earth and white sand where the Gulf of Carpentaria meets the emerald water of the Arafura Sea at Gove.

— In the shadow of the monstrous bauxite mining plant Aborigines cling desperately to tradition. A personal view of a ceremony mourning the death of an ancestor spirit, returned in the form of a crocodile, shot for killing a European.

Like an infestation of millipedes tracking across a vast empty pan of red and yellow ochres, rivers worm through the hirsute coast of mangroves. From ten thousand feet it is a fascinating abstraction of patterns; back to earth it is in fact the arid habitation of crocodiles – spare a thought for Ludwig Leichhardt.

Odd rectangular clearings are the only evidence of man. The abandoned war-time airstrips today facilitate the running of contraband such as drugs.

No road leads to Gove so we have taken the four hour flight from Darwin to the north-east tip of Arnhem Land where the Arafura Sea meets the waters of the Gulf of Carpentaria.

From the serenity of this height it is difficult to relate to the terrain below. Movement across the flood plains, deep tidal rivers and steeply banked creeks is hazardous in the dry — impossible in the wet. Under humid tropical conditions keeping food is a constant problem. Leichhardt spared no thought for his personal comfort but his diary records: " ..... oppressed by hunger I swallowed the bones and feet of a pigeon to allay the cravings of my stomach. A sleeping lizard with a blunt tail and knobby scales, fell into our hands, and was of course roasted and greedily eaten ..... two wallabies, which were stewed, and to which I added some green hide to render the broth more substantial. This hide was almost five months old, and had served as a case to my botanical collection which, unfortunately, I had been compelled to leave behind. It required, however, a little longer stewing than a fresh hide, and was rather tasteless". On another occasion from the crop of a cockatoo he recovered and ate fruits resembling grains of rice. Among Australia's early explorers Ludwig Leichhardt was the most adept at living off the land. He would try anything once. Such as the fruit of the pandanus palm. Without the knowledge Aborigines have of treating this fruit before eating he suffered sore lips, a blistered tongue and severe diarrhoea.

Twenty years after Leichhardt was lost without a trace of his final resting place another bearded giant, John McKinlay, survived a shorter but frustrating journey across the swampy plains. Though veteran of many successful expeditions, this time he failed to do his homework. Ignoring the predictable weather pattern of the north he set out with fourteen men, forty five horses and a mob of sheep from Escape Cliffs, near the mouth of the Adelaide River, in January 1866. Plans for a relatively short journey of exploration were thwarted by the late January north-west monsoons. From the start horses bogged down and it was a matter of days only when the expedition was completely marooned. For six

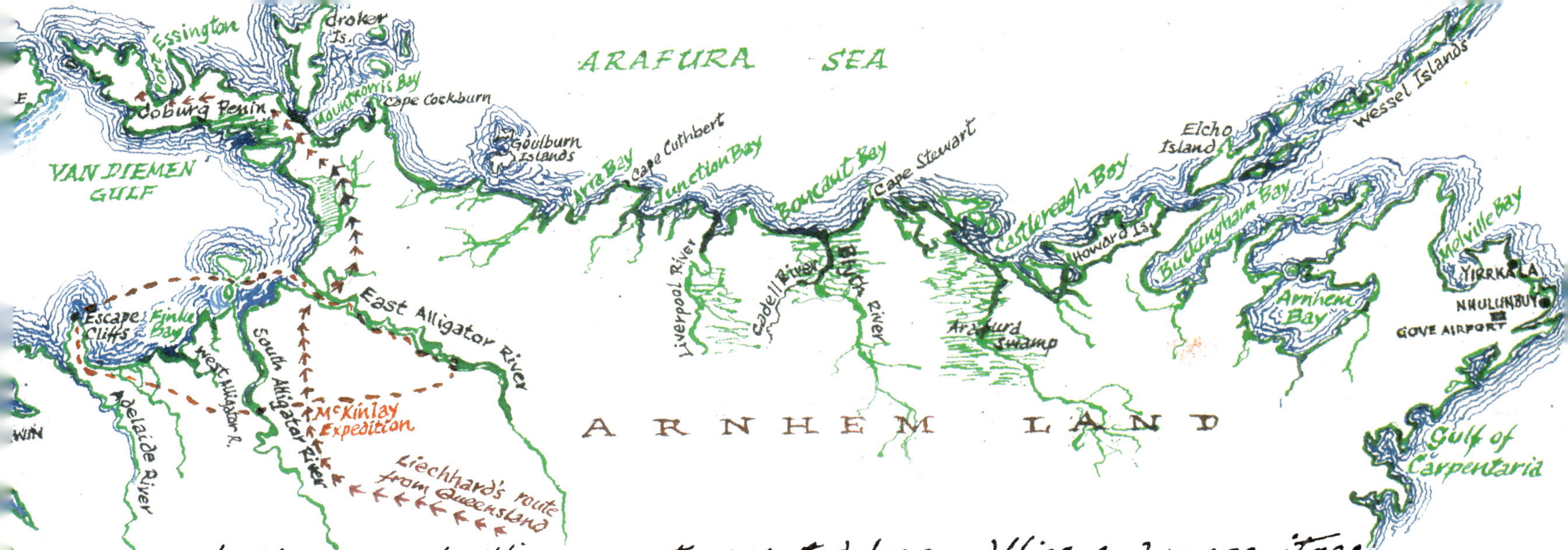

tedious weeks they were tormented by sandflies and mosquitoes. Each day more horses and sheep died while the surviving animals suffered the barbs of grass seeds and attacks by crocodiles. To conserve supplies the party experimented with crocodile eggs and prepared a stew of flying foxes, a dish which became known as 'curried vampire'. As varied cuisine they ate horse meat. As they floundered through swamps to the East Alligator River McKinlay's men were attacked by Aborigines. Though by the time his party had reached the river the monsoons had decreased and the plains were drying out McKinlay decided to return by sea. To achieve this a seven metre raft was constructed of saplings and covered with the hides of the remaining horses. While the raft was being loaded with horse flesh and fresh water the party was again attacked by Aborigines.

The hides which made the raft buoyant attracted scores of crocodiles. Their open jawed lunges and ferocious snapping rent many holes in the craft, causing two men to bail frantically, while eight others propelled it with hide covered paddles; the splash and smell of these proved even more attractive to the crocodiles.

Clearing the mangroves at the mouth of the East Alligator the raft was blown far offshore to spin around and around in the open sea. None of the crew had any sailing experience and most were violently seasick. During six days at sea supplies of fresh water were exhausted and the only food was putrifying horse meat, eaten raw. The stench of this and the horse hides, which were decaying rapidly, aroused the curiosity of sharks, though they did not attack.

The raft fell to pieces as the survivors staggered ashore at Escape Cliffs. All the sheep had been lost early in the expedition and of the forty five horses only a few returned as rotting hides. All fifteen men lived to tell their versions of the experience but McKinlay's fine reputation as an explorer was lost.

The coastal fringe of mangroves clears to expose sandy beaches and clear lagoons along Gove Peninsula. Behind the white sand is bauxite red. Even the strip we land on is bauxite and that too will be mined and shipped out.

None of our fellow passengers is a tourist. All are connected in some way with the mining. Apart from the beaches there is little to attract tourists and sea-wasps menace these tropical waters for seven months of the year.

The tiny airport building is stifling and packed with yelling locals, yet the flashed grins, loud laughter and chatter of Aboriginal greeting is infectious. The glassy blue-black skin and high cheek bones bond these north-eastern Arnhem Landers in a family likeness, though some are stocky, even obese, while others carry well developed, slim hipped bodies on long sinewy legs like stilting birds.

The waiting vehicles load quickly and disappear noisily to leave us inhaling exhaust fumes in a forlorn silence. The lone taxi has a fare to Yirrkala but the driver assures us a lift on his way back to Nhulunbuy. In the timeless north an hour this way or that matters little but we soon find that Goveans add thirty minutes to an hour on to the acceptable time lapse.

At three in the afternoon an official cheerfully turfs us out of the reception building saying, "Time to lock up." Passing through the door to shelterless heat I observe that this has to be the most expensive and uncomfortable line and the least courteous service of all time, anywhere. He grins in reply, "There is another, in New Guinea, and that's not so far from here." Asked again about 'phoning a cab he informs us that there are only two and the other driver is off playing football. In this climate the game is inconceivable. Moving with our gear to keep the building between ourselves and the sun we sweat out the second mandatory hour.

At last the cab shows up and, perhaps, by way of apology the driver remarks, "Had a couple of fares back to Nhulunbuy and out to Yirrkala since I saw you."

The bitumen cuts through a flatness of red bauxite and wind beaten olive green scrub to the satellite mining town of Nhulunbuy and its modern motel, the Walk-about. The club bar is a cave-like haven after the squinting glare of the heat outside. And the air-conditioned bedroom has shower, television and telephone — highly civilized this frontier life.

But time and place are re-affirmed by an attempt to 'phone the Community Centre of Yirrkala, the neighbouring Aboriginal settlement. 'Engaged,' says our receptionist, 'I'll try again'. This patient lady perservered for an hour before she got a positive ring. I ask for Wandjuk Marika. 'Not here,' answers a thick throaty voice with child-like simplicity. 'Where can I get him?' I ask. 'Don't know,' from gravel voice. 'But everyone here must know Wandjuk, he's a famous artist,' I insist. 'Yeah, but not here,' deep throat persists. I press him to find Wandjuk and what must be ten minutes later he enlightens me with, 'in Canberra'. Of course, he is currently Chairman of the Aboriginal Arts Board. 'Perhaps you can help me. I want to look around Yirrkala'. I plead. 'You need permit.' 'Where do I get it?' 'Not here, you get permit first.' 'Yes but where?' 'Nhulunbuy Land Council'. Though the telephone meter is ticking away at least I haven't wasted the expensive cab fare and suffered the one and a half hour wait.

The Northern Land Council are more articulate but no more helpful about the permit. 'What do you want to see in Yirrkala?' asks the lady. 'I don't know what's there, so how do I know till I see it,' I explain, 'I'm a painter and want to make some sketches.' She is not impressed so I suggest seeing her; it is just across the street from the hotel. 'Come tomorrow, it's nearly four and we're finished for the day,' she concluded. Mañana por la mañana, how often I heard that in Spain and found the morrow to be another fiesta day.

Fellow traveller and painter David Dridan and I filled in the late afternoon taking in the town, Government offices, Town Hall, Police Station, Public Library, Hospital with Flying Doctor Service, Primary and High Schools and sizable shopping centre, all modern buildings but without character. The land belongs to the Yirrala based Aborigines and is leased to Nabalco for 99 years then to be handed back in its original condition. Traditional Aboriginal thinking is opposed to large communities but when the time comes they will be reluctant to give up the town's amenities which have become a large part of their life style. Alcohol presents the all too familiar problems but the Aborigines themselves attempt to control the sale of it. The bottle shop sells them only one can of beer at a time and the empty can must be returned before another is sold. This also solves a litter problem.

The club opposite the Walkabout has been recommended but we find it smoked up and crowded so retreat to the relative peace of the hotel. At dinner the wide choice of dishes surprises since every morsel is flown in, even the barramundi whose delicate flavour has survived refrigeration. And the buffalo steak is as tender and succulent as it should be.

Relaxed after a comfortable night we settle into a cab ordered an hour and a half earlier and head back to the airport road junction to Yirrkala. The bitumen connecting the mining plant and the town of Nhulunbuy does not extend to Yirrkala, about twenty five minutes drive. The road is bauxite but will be bitumen after it has been mined. Red bauxite crystal is weathered rock which has developed naturally over perhaps a hundred thousand years in tropical conditions. Alumina is produced from this ore and the Gove deposit is a rich one; three kilograms of bauxite processes one kilogram of aluminium.

The monotony of the landscape is broken only by signs of new growth pushing up through the red earth. The driver tells us this area has already been mined. A metre deep of topsoil and vegetation had been removed for the operation and afterwards replaced along with native trees and shrubs seeded before the last wet set in. It is said this restoration has already attracted animals and birds back to the area and species previously unfamiliar locally have appeared.

Equipped with one-day-only passes we approach the Community Centre or Council Chambers, a simple timber frame fibro building, two rooms joined by an open verandah and perched on the rail children yell happily at yelping dogs. In one of the rooms we find a slim blue-black young man in khaki shirt and shorts sitting behind a school desk; there is a simple wooden bench for visitors. We produce the permits and explain that we would like to sketch the local landscape. Taking us behind the building which backs onto the beach he points saying "You can go one hundred metres up the beach or one hundred down, no more. And those people

down there," pointing towards a bunch of kids aged five to twelve years splashing merrily in a lagoon, "don't take any photos! They may not like it." Well beyond this inlet and camping on the ocean beach under a bright blue plastic tarpaulin a party of adults are so distant they look like tiny black ants foraging in the white sand around a blue nest.

The sea is emerald inshore blending to azure and ultramarine closer to the cloudless sky. Too beautiful to paint so I make some sketches of 'those people down there', feeling no guilt. After all, sketches are not photographs.

Another sketch is touched off by a narrow spit of land supporting a vehicle track which sweeps in a gentle curve out through the ocean to disappear in hazy infinity. Mid afternoon we retrace our steps over the restricted hundred metres of beach to ask the 'boss' what else we may see. He appears to be pondering this but instead asks, "What do you do with those sketches?" "Paint pictures from them," we reply. "When you finish with one I'd like to have it," he said graciously.

More relaxed now he offers to drive us around to some of the other beaches when his cousin returns the truck. His cousin, however, proves to be less friendly and asks contemptuously, "You got permit? How long you stay?" Obviously the truck is not available to us so we call Nhulunbuy for a cab. The Yirrkala Arts Centre, well subsidised by the Aboriginal Arts Board to encourage the production and sale of local art, is closed today so we while away the taxi waiting hour watching

the children play in the palmy shade of the old Methodist mission homestead.

No longer a mission Yirrkala has raised its own defences against outside influences of evil. Its proximity to Nhulunbuy has led to economic disruption and increased alcoholism. Yirrkala itself is strictly dry. The entire spaciality of Aboriginal minds and customs centres on small communities and a nomadic life style. They were opposed to the establishment of Nhulunbuy which now houses 3,500 people, the third largest town in the Northern Territory. In a direct attack on mining exploitation in 1968 the Aboriginal Land Council protested the excision of 330 square kilometres of land owned by the people of Yirrkala. Their claims of traditional ownership were refused by the Northern Territory Supreme Court and the Federal Government. With Government approval NABALCO set up the processing plant at Melville Bay and built the town of Nhulunbuy in the early 1970s. It was not till 1976 that Aboriginal ownership of this land was recognised. They now receive royalties of $1.000.000 plus $50,000 for leases each year. A substantial portion of this is paid to the Yirrkala community and the balance is used for the benefit of all Aborigines of the Northern Territory.

Since mining began Aboriginal movement to their clan outstations has gathered impetus. This has opened up a way of distancing themselves and rehabilitating their traditional way of life. On walkabout from outstations Aborigines collect stringy bark for painting, milkwood for carving and rush corms for eating which they trade at Yirrkala. Runways are cleared by the outstation communities and chartered flights are made by the Missionary Aviation Fellowship and medical personnel. Clans own defined areas of land and the ritual knowledge and objects associated with it. Though rarely in permanent occupation they return to their outstations to perform sacred ceremonies known as Mardyin. Totemism forms the basis of solidarity within the clans.

Yirrkala children splash merrily in a tiny lagoon. Though narrowly channeled to the Arafura Sea the lagoon offers a degree of safety from seawasps, sharks and crocodiles.

Hunting and gathering was the way of life among north-east Arnhem Landers until the late 1930s. Hand-outs from the missions set up at Milingimbi (1922), Yirrkala (1934) and Elcho Island (1944) have made Aboriginals increasingly dependant upon sugar and flour. These replaced their natural staples — native honey and yams or corms of the mat-rush which grows on the edge of salt pans. Eaten raw the corm, known locally as rakay, is about the size of a hazel nut and tastes much the same. Yams are roasted in the ashes, the skin then rubbed off and the tuber sliced and soaked for some hours. Squeezed to a pulp it looks and tastes like sweet mashed potato.

A delicacy also roasted in ashes is the goose egg; particularly relished are those taken shortly before hatching!

Geese were hunted in mosquito infested brackish waters such as the Arafura Swamp of the Glyde River. In search of goose eggs hunters poled through the thickly grassed swamp in fragile canoes of stringy-bark, each made from a single folded sheet, smoked to prevent cracking, the nose and stern sewn with fibre and caulked with clay. In open water these light canoes were speedy when paddled with the hands from a sitting position.

The Methodist missions pleaded tolerance towards Aboriginal ritual and ceremony. Their professed objectives were to encourage integration with white society through education and to encourage self sufficiency through agriculture and craft. Ironically, their indigenous economy, which had evolved and worked well for many thousands of years, had been destroyed by that of the evangelical white man. They now had to buy things which had previously belonged to everyone.

Even so, the impact of European influence remained minimal until the 1960s when the discovery of bauxite on the Gove Peninsular dramatically changed the scene. Yirrkala, gathering point for the Yolngu linguistic group, is located in the very centre of the mineral deposit.

For one hundred and twenty years after Matthew Flinders visited Caledon Bay, while mapping the coast of Arnhem Land in 1803, European contact in that vast unknown was limited to isolated encounters with explorers and mineral prospectors. Yet disease previously unknown in this area caused depopulation in the 19th century. During this period the coast was frequented by Indonesian fishermen. Sailing from Macassar with the North West gales that herald the 'wet' they returned the following year in March-April when the winds swung to the South East. An indication of the extent of the annual invasion was given by Flinders in his encounter with six praus in a sheltered strait later named Malay Road. The Pobasso, commander of the fishing expedition, told Flinders there were no less than sixty praus operating along the coast at that time, all owned by the Sultan of Boni, with crews totalling about one thousand. They came to collect pearl and turtle shell and to gather trepang, a sea-slug also known as beche-de-mer. Back in the trading port of Macassar trepang was prized by Chinese merchants and sold as a delicacy and aphrodisiac.

Aboriginal groups helped collect, dry and cure trepang in smoke-houses built on shore and traded pearl and turtle shell for the Indonesians' dug-out canoes, tobacco and clothing.

The Macassans became so much part of community life that to this day their visits, which ceased eighty years ago, are sung and mimed. Pennants representing the sails of praus are displayed in ceremonies. In burial ritual these symbolise farewell.

from a Wuramu carving of a Macassan. ht. approx. 1m

Although Indonesian contact over two or three centuries had little impact on the basic structure of Aboriginal society, along with such advantages as iron, the dug-out canoe and the long-stemmed pipe they did introduce yaws, smallpox, leprosy, venereal disease and, though Muslim, they used alcohol freely. As a possible result of contamination by the Macassan sailors

Macassan prau.
. from a Groote Eylandt bark painting

the women of Groote Eylandt were secluded. Till recent years when mission influence altered their tabus no male stranger was allowed to see their women. Doubling as a screen a wrap-around garment of tea-tree bark was worn. Made in two vertical sections it was hinged to be a free-standing hide when placed in an angled position. A further restriction on girls at that time was the ritual of circumcision.

1907 Federal legislation banned the Indonesian intruders but Japanese fishermen continued to gather trepang along that coast and to increase the incidence of venereal disease, then recorded as epidemic throughout the Eastern world. From the beach at Mooroonga Island in the Crocodile group Donald Thomson, the anthropologist, observed a fleet of more than seventy Japanese pearling luggers in 1937. One of these was crewed by fifteen men. Conservatively he calculated the flotilla's complement as seven hundred.
Lured by gifts of tobacco, fish hooks and knives Aboriginals suspended normal activities and gathered at various watering places between Elcho Island and Cape Stewart. Prostitution of women, even little girls, flourished.
Aboriginal resentment of the violation of their women peaked in 1932 with the killing of five Japanese at Caledon Bay. A police punitive expedition, to teach the offending Aboriginals a lesson they would never forget, was replaced by a 'peace mission' organised by missionaries to bring the culprits to Darwin ostensibly for conciliatory talks but in fact to be arrested and tried for murder. Evidence was given in court that the crews of two Japanese luggers, illegally poaching on the reserve, had built a smoke-house on shore, had taken and held Aboriginal women in that house under armed guard and had beaten the men who attempted to rescue the women. Three of the accused, sons of Wongo, revered elder of the Balamumu of Caledon and Trial Bays, were sentenced to twenty years hard labour in Fannie Bay gaol.
This incident and the killing of two white trepang fishermen

under similar circumstances at Woodah Island, Blue Mud Bay made headlines in Sydney and Melbourne. On Woodah broken glass was scattered around the mission as defence against the 'bare-foot army' thought to be massing on the mainland at Blue Mud Bay. The press predicted war in Australia. A strong force of police was expedited to the area in 1933. One of its constables, McColl, was killed, not in line of duty but in a domestic fight with Takiara, an Aboriginal. Found guilty of murder in the Supreme Court Takiara was sentenced to death, though witnesses had sworn that McColl had first handcuffed Takiara's wife then raped her; later he had emptied his revolver at Takiara as he approached to his wife's call for help.

Public outcry pressured the Federal Government to resolve the crisis on the Northern frontier. Choosing between forceful and peaceful means it accepted Donald Thomson's proposal of a single unarmed man's approach. He wanted to demonstrate "the practical value of an anthropological approach to avert disaster" and to pave the way for reform in the administration of Aboriginal affairs.

Thomson found the Caledon Bay Aboriginals "kindly, warm and gentle". Wongo was handed a message stick from his sons, gaoled in Darwin and told that the big country government, displeased with the killings, wanted him to keep his people peaceful. In accepting responsibility he presented to Thomson a message stick with incisions indicating himself sitting and maintaining peace.

Years later, during World War II, in Command of the Special Reconnaissance Force Thomson returned to Caledon Bay, again to enlist Wongo's good-will. Sporting a vanDyke beard (side whiskers pulled with the black wax of native bees) Wongo greeted him like a son. Thomson was aware of the irony of the situation as he told Wongo that the big country government now wanted to recruit his people to kill Japanese. Wongo offered five of his six sons present, including the three who had been gaoled (now released) for killing five Japanese. Only one of the sons was sceptical of this licence to kill.

From Cape Stewart to Blue Mud Bay and along the Koolatong River the sixty and more clans which form the Yolngu linguistic group speak many dialects; some are so mutually unintelligible as to be different languages, though many clan elders are multi lingual.

The Yolngu are divided into two halves, two Moieties called the Dhuwa and the Yirritja. All beings natural and supernatural, all things animate and inanimate, animal species, plants, the winds and even colours belong to one or the other moiety, never to both. The Dhuwa owns red ochre and white and the Yirritja moiety claims yellow ochre and black; these are traded between groups.

No two clans have the same set of totemic species; each clan owns defined areas of land and the Madayin or sacred law associated with it — expressed in songs, dances, paintings and sacred objects. Their songs recall the everyday happenings experienced by Ancestor beings on their creation journeys — fighting, giving birth and such mundane activities as eating, sleeping or simply observing a feature in the landscape such as a split in a rock.

A person belonging to a clan of the Yirritja moiety must marry someone of the Dhuwa. Marriages are arranged by close relatives.

The moieties have different ancestor figures from whom all the laws and rules governing life are derived.

Creation of the Angurugwa River, Groote Eylandt. →

From a painting on bark by Nandabita of the Andiljangwa group.

The mythic sawfish formed the river by sawing a cut through the land. It is shown with stingrays and sharkrays credited with creating nearby sites.

Consistent to their belief that all creatures and beings are related metamorphosis from human to animal and back to human is part of Aboriginal spiritual understanding.
The origin of fire has intrigued man since the beginning — the Dreamtime; and each clan has its own myth. Various birds have been revered for creating fire, others have stolen it only to have it taken from them by man. In Arnhem Land many clans accept the crocodile as "boss for fire". The story below comes from Oenpelli.

Two hunters were stalking waterfowl while their mothers gathered waterlily bulbs and seeds. The women had knowledge of fire but cherished the secret. Surprised by the returning hunters while cooking lily-cake they hid the live coals in their vulvas. Knowing the women had fire the hunters argued that they should have it to cook their catch and so prevent it going bad. Eventually the men found that by rubbing two sticks together fire was theirs. They decided to become crocodiles. With pounded and fired bark they fashioned heads then pierced their lungs to enable breathing under water.

When the women who had set nets to fish tried to pull them in the men had a firm hold and pulled the women into the water to drown. The men then perfected their crocodile transformation and kept the secret of fire.

In a legend from the Dabaln the crocodile jealously guarded fire in the form of fire sticks. When the Rainbow bird's request for fire was refused it swooped down from a tall tree to snatch the sticks. Finally succeeding the Rainbow bird put fire inside every tree making it available to man. And that is why the land is always burnt out. The bird placed the sticks in his behind where they feature to this day. And the crocodile retreated to the water where he needed no fire.

In this illustration (after a bark painting from the Gumaitj clan of Gove Peninsula) Bäru, the crocodile ancestor, bringer of fire, is set in a geometrical pattern of spreading fire.

The primeval appearance and menacing nature of the saltwater crocodile has stimulated wide interpretation among graphic artists. Images of tremendous vitality have been created by Aboriginals and children. A child's fresh approach to drawing — "I think and then I put a line around my think." — produced this telling image.

Alongside this, separated from the innocent eye by centuries of seeing, the Aboriginal painting of a crocodile (opposite) is sophisticated. As a traditional rendering of ancestor mythology, painted again for today's bäru totem ceremony, it could be said to be academic.

Norman Fisher
Mary River Station
via Pine Creek
Grade 3
KATHERINE SCHOOL OF THE AIR
P.O. BOX 531
KATHERINE, N.T. 5780

One such ancestor being rose from the sea at Blue Mud Bay. Patterns of water glistened on the body of this original creator, Laindjung, and these formed the sacred designs of the Yirridja moiety. In some of the many myths Barama, who emerged from a nearby waterhole at much the same time, was the 'real big boss' and Laindjung, a wayward disciple, publicly broadcast secret knowledge of designs and sang sacred songs to the uninitiated. Speared to death for his sins Laindjung rose from a watery grave to be transformed into a paper-bark tree (dhulwu).

Of the Dhuwa moiety this djuwei post represents the elder of the Wawilak Sisters, great ancestors who created North East Arnhem Land. This post is danced around during djunggawon circumcision ritual. The vertical pattern of dots on the head depicts pebbles walked over by the Wawilak sisters in their epic journeys before they were swallowed by the python Yulunggul. Below the hair, which is stringy bark left on the carved trunk, is a design of ridjangu berries and leaves. String around the hair are feathered pendants. Stone spear-heads and their timber mountings form the lower part of the design.

From a wood carving with painted Yirridja moiety design and headdress of featherdown with string pendants. Ht. approx 1m.

A similar carving of the great mythic personage Laindjung, or Banaidja, is among those displayed in the Elcho Island Memorial, focal point of an attempt to integrate religion in Arnhem Land and to show the people that politics and administration are working efficiently for the Aboriginal community in the whole area.

Traditional stylized human figures such as these have developed over thousands of years. Some are burial posts used in mortuary ritual, others are derived from sacred rangga emblems. Both are so interwoven with the powerful mythic cycles that it is difficult to separate one from the other.

Looking across Melville Bay from the white sandy beach an incongruous monument of towers, conveyor belts and tall chimney stacks rises like an industrial Parthenon. The horizon is smudged a smoky red from the bauxite processing plant built in the early 1970's by the Swiss/Australian consortium of companies, Nabalco. Without dredging the bay can accommodate ships of 100,000 tonnes.

On the 'phone T.A.A. representative Terry Simpson had promised us a grand tour of the area. We dally an hour of this brilliant morning in the hotel lobby studying each arrival, because we have yet to meet Terry, then mention his name to the manager. "Old Gonna?" he quips, then explains, "He's always gonna do something for you." On the obligatory hour and a half we are about to pack it in and settle for the local beach when he came through the entrance, quite a bit of the morning's sun scorched into his fair complexion. No apology showed on his brightly polished, cheerful round face.

A run around suburbia here reminds me of retirement towns, holiday resorts along many coasts down south, boats on trailers, modern bungalows, blocks of units, manicured lawns and gardens, but the odd buffalo grazing on the nature strip identifies the locale.

Passing under the towering conveyor belt (one of the largest in the world) which carries the bauxite to the processing plant Terry explains that the wives of the thousand or so company employees are encouraged to work, some even drive the big trucks — Terry points to a whopper capable of carrying 85 tonnes. Few Aborigines, on the other hand, are employed at the works; steady routine is not their life style.

Answering my query about problems between the Company and Aborigines he points to a banyan tree just beyond a tall wire fence saying, "Two office blocks were built near that tree. The Aborigines then declared the tree so sacred that nothing should be close to it, so the buildings were moved."

"And about violence?" "The local blacks are pretty quiet," replies Terry, "I've only been hit twice by them and that was refereeing football. They take the game seriously. Ofcourse when some of them drink it's another scene."

I ask about drugs or brews from native substances. "Kava" he explains, "but that's smuggled in from Fiji by barge in 500 kilo containers. It's a powder you mix with water, tastes like soapy bath water; numbs the lips, makes your toes tingle and the legs go wobbly. The Aborigines get sleepy on it and even if the odd one was aggressive he couldn't stand up.

A spit of sand between two lagoons leads to the ocean near East Woody Beach.
Popular at weekends this weekday it is unbelievably tranquil.

It is currently reported that missionaries on Elcho Island have been importing kava and actually capitalising on its sale to Aborigines, the justification being that it is less harmful than beer. But the womenfolk say kava turns their men into useless layabouts who don't come home for days.

Leaving the car on the edge of loose sand we walk along Shady Beach towards a magnificent Beauty Leaf tree. Time has seen many problems thrashed out in the generous shade of this tree. It has come to be known as the conference tree and was the site for recent talks between clan elders and Clyde Holding, Federal Minister for Aboriginal Affairs.

Closer to Nhulunbuy East Woody Beach is popular but this weekday it is unbelievably tranquil. Pausing under a banyan tree I attempt the impossible, to record this serenity; paradise tarnished by the scatter of beer cans and plastic bags.

The timelessness of the next beach we visit had been arrested in 1944-45 by 5000 personnel of the R.A.A.F. A base for flying boats, the Catalina from which the beach takes its name, was established here. Rusted fuel drums and a bitumen surfaced launching ramp are the unattractive legacies of World War II. But, Terry points out, Gulurruy Yunupingu finds the site useful. He plans to build a waterfront house and use the ramp for slipping his boat. If it is the one moored offshore it is an impressive yacht, built for blue water sailing. With royalties from the mining an educated head man can afford luxuries, and some that white men may not, such as four wives. But his integrity is not doubted by his people, who are encouraged to maintain their traditions, their rites, songs and dances. When Gulurruy was deposed as Chairman of the Northern Land Council a few years ago he was undecided about nominating for re-election, then had a dream about a cyclone in which his children were endangered in the mangroves. His personal symbol is the stingray, Gufumo, an ancestor celebrated for protecting his young. This omen decided Gulurruy to stand again for the Chairmanship and he was elected.

The clear turquoise water is tempting but Terry warns of sea-wasps, a painful killer which menaces tropical waters from October to May. "Sharks are no great problem but you see a few crocs," Terry goes on, "mostly in the mangroves, but a nest with eggs was found on the beach a couple of weeks ago. They keep a close eye on their nests; its the most dangerous time with crocs. Mostly they take dogs and an occasional black but a white was killed a few years ago, a guy who tried to take a photograph of a crocodile under water. He didn't surface so his mates alerted the police. They found his body intact, except for a broken arm, tucked away in the mangroves. Crocs don't like fresh meat so they store their victims away until they are good and gamey. It was easy to find the guilty croc because they are territorial, almost every day each croc covers the same ground. Crocs are protected so a team of conservationists were flown in to remove this one along with two others to the farm near Darwin for breeding purposes. But the Chief Minister heard about the croc which drowned the photographer and ordered that it be shot. It was shot in the head but not fatally; the bullet lifted the cranium, throwing the croc out of whack. They say it was chasing its tail for a day or so before given the coup de grâce. Its carcass was left on the beach as a warning to both foolhardy skindivers and wayward crocodiles.

The local Aboriginal clans, the Gumaitj and the Madarrpa, were upset by the killing because crocodiles represent ancestor totems and are sacred to them. It was of even greater concern to Gulurruy Yunupingu because the spirit of his father, who had died shortly before, had passed into this particular crocodile, which he had fed regularly. To appease the offended spirit the Darwin Museum is having the totem stuffed for return to its people."

Back in Darwin Ian Archibald had a dossier on the crocodile. It was shot on the 7th October 1979. From teeth to tail 3·900 metres, it measured 1·560 metres across the shoulders and only 36 centimetres down through the belly. Though skinny its shoulders were broad. No food was found in its stomach, just three plastic bags from Woolworths. ('Sweetheart', the six metre estuarine on display in the Museum, had been full of game; whole wallaby, leg of buffalo and plenty of barramundi). Shortage of freezing chambers had made taxidermy difficult and the smell had been appalling. A search for artificial crocodile eyes had proved fruitless. The demand for these curiosities does not warrant their manufacture anywhere in the world. Finally a pair of ruby red glass alligator eyes were imported from Florida, U.S.A. Though Ian did not know if the crocodile had an Aboriginal pet name he said Dave Lindner had dubbed it Cuthbert. There is a river named Cuthbert on the north coast.

Now completely restored and wrapped in plastic the lamented Cuthbert was awaiting the revelation of his return to the people of Gove. In fact he had returned already to Melville Bay, but secretly; he was smuggled in and hidden away in a Company store. Too large for regular flights he had been carried on the first available large aircraft to put down at Gove.

The mortuary ceremony planned for the return of this great ancestor totem had been postponed many times. As the months passed into a year and more Archibald feared for Cuthbert's wellbeing. Rats could be tearing him to pieces, termites systematically chewing from the inside or perhaps maggots were at work in his gums. The gums, Ian told me, are difficult to cure; for some time they harbour maggots. When 'Sweetheart' was exhibited fainthearted visitors to the newly built Museum swooned at the repulsive sight of maggots active inside the gaping jaws.

The Gumaitj and Madarrpa at last got their act

together. Elaborate dilly bags were woven of pandanus fibre with tassels of red breast feathers of the rainbow lorikeet, bark was painted with totem images and patterns and a crocodile effigy was carved of milkwood. Dance and mime were rehearsed and the date was set for the 16th June 1985. It had taken six years but there is no rush on the Gove Peninsula.

Soon after landing on June 15th we searched for Gulurruy Yunupingu and found him on Catalina Beach rehearsing his performers. His torso is a superbly polished blue-black but, sadly, he soon covered it with a shirt. He discussed the following day's procedure with Colin Jack-Hinton and agreed that the 'curtain' should be raised at noon.

A short drive away at Melville Beach we met Cabbage, the man whose boat Colin wanted to hire for the crocodile lift to Catalina Beach. Nobody seemed to know his real name. I had heard it was Elvis Presley and he grinned at the suggestion saying, "Something like that, just call me Cabbage". His roguish but friendly face is Nordic and topped by a striped stocking cap or beanie. A full sandy beard tumbles from his chin. He remarks that odd cargo keeps him in business; he picked up a corpse on the point the other day and delivered it at Nhulunbuy. Colin asks the going rate for stuffed crocodiles. Cabbage replies that he doesn't discriminate, it's the same as for humans, fifty bucks.

Cabbage has a tiny shadow — a son of three years who follows him everywhere. Saying little, he keeps an eye on everything. Even before his father had moved to push the dinghy into the water he hopped aboard. The family, along with father-in-law, live on a large trawler moored well out in the bay. Tied up alongside is a Vietnamese fishing lugger, the 'Ken Tueng', which Cabbage has been restoring. Above its black hull the cabin and superstructure has been freshly painted a bold red.

blue and white. Built in 1974 from 30 cubic metres of timber, all solid, Cabbage explained, because plywood is expensive in Vietnam, each of the hull planks was shaped and clamped by eye and the ribs positioned later, the opposite process to that of Europe, and joined by wooden dowel. The Ken Tueng arrived in Darwin in October 1977 with forty three 'boat people' on its small deck after what must have been a hellish 2000 miles from South-east Vietnam to Singapore then south to Faulkner Point and Darwin, navigated by simple compass and a school atlas of Malaysia, New Guinea and the north coast of Australia. It had been impounded by the authorities, as have about fifty other similar Vietnamese luggers. Cabbage had bought it for a couple of hundred dollars, but import duty ran into thousands. His registration as a professional fisherman reduced this sum considerably.

Nosing into every cove and river deep enough to float the lugger Cabbage and family explored the coast from Darwin to Gove. During the five months voyage they lived off the sea; crayfish, barramundi and oysters were the daily staples. An enviable life-style till those big black clouds herald a monsoon – or a cyclone.

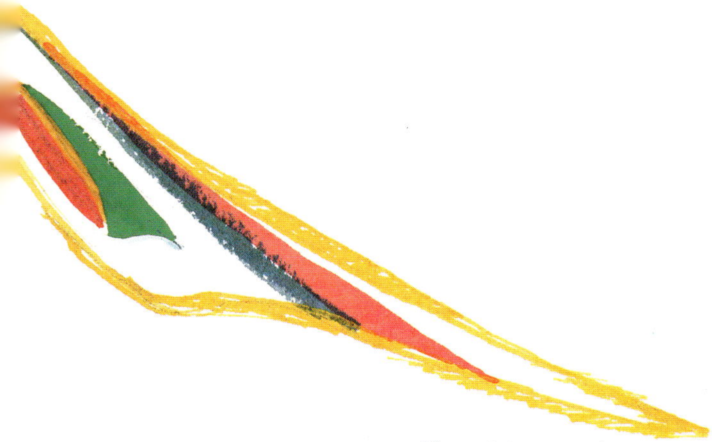

The all-seeing eye of the Ken Tueng

and the face of its wheel-house

In plastic shroud Cuthbert occupied four metres of the five metre boat leaving just enough space for Cabbage and son to swing the tiller and the pallbearers to perch on the gunwale. Beards whipped by a stiff breeze they pushed off at 10 a.m. in choppy water. Crocodile landing time had been set for noon. Though Cabbage had calculated sailing time at thirty minutes in the roughest of seas Colin, both a navy and army officer, had planned a fail-safe operation and cautioned against possible white or black man's voodooism; the team sheltered on the eastern headland of Catalina Beach where they unwrapped the crocodile cadaver and shivered out the hour and a half in a surprisingly bitter wind.

A pervading spooky blue-grey, the ceremonial ground and sky are separated by a sliver of azure sea. Plastered from hair to heel with blue-grey mangrove mud the performers merge with the bitumen surface of the wartime launching ramp. The dancers are limbering up and forming groups, some in file, others curving to form a 'U'. Wandjuk Marika, elder, painter and presently ballet master, seems determined to put them through certain dance routines. Wearing a headband of red and white diamond pattern, white beard falling on to a crisp white shirt, maroon pullover and brown slacks with polished shoes he is an incongruous figure among his near naked and mud splattered people. His directional gestures have all the assertion of a symphony orchestra conductor but the dancers pay little heed. Some musicians claim that a good orchestra needs no conductor. Masters of the spontaneous gesture this line-up of individuals does seem to perform better without formal restrictions; instinctively a dancer picks up the rhythmic movement as another performer fades out, rekindles it and moves in a new routine.

The audience is swelling to near one hundred and fifty. Spreading sheets on the ground the blacks squat in colourful groups outnumbering the whites sitting uncomfortably on rows of metal chairs. Clapping sticks and hands children are performing an impromptu ceremony. From birth dance and mime are an integral part of their daily life.

As they grow they are taught childrens dances and on initiation the more complicated and meaningful ritual steps are revealed to them. Audience participation is part of the performance; not everyone plays an individual role but all join in chanting and clapping.

Staged in theatre Aboriginal ritual performances are not convincing; enclosed space inhibits these people. They need the vastness of the universe, their living space, to perform in; in a state of oneness with their landscape, a deeply rooted spirituality, inherited knowledge is released.

A rope barrier between audience and performers supports six large bark paintings. These and a one and a half metre wood carving of a crocodile are painted with Yolgnu ritual designs relating to the baru ceremony. Some are representational, others are geometrical abstractions such as diamond pattern which represents the fire which this celebrated crocodile brought to the people. And this explains the three piles of dry grass nearby.

The didjeridu drones, sticks are clapped, dancers leap and actors flex their spear throwing muscles while spectators shout above the chatter and laughter. Suddenly all are hushed as the crocodile carrier rounds the headland.

On a grass tufted dune between bitumen and beach the performers prostrate themselves. Stealthily, like a crocodile out of water, the leading man gyrates his body as though his navel is balanced on a pivot.

In shallow water a few metres away the four white pall-bearers lift the totem body from the boat and carry it ashore. With an ear piercing shriek the blacks leap to their feet swinging clubs and brandishing long quivering spears. (The leading pallbearers Jack-Hinton and Chaloupka, said later that the surprise confrontation was: 'spine chilling' and 'bloody terrifying').

Threatening with his spear an actor cautiously approaches to look closely at the crocodile then backs off. Another repeats this performance while the main body slowly retreats before the advancing crocodile party.

Two powerfully built dancers, one with a heavy fighting club, the other brandishing a smaller club and long quivering spear, dance to the edge of the ceremonial ground and, back to back, make challenging gestures at things or beings hidden in the landscape. They turn, apparently surprised, and threaten one another, then just as suddenly turn again aggressively to mutually attack an unseen enemy.

In mime and dance the action is electric. As among jazz musicians one sequence touches off another so these natural actors and dancers perform their ritual. The changes in rhythmic movements appear so spontaneous you are not conscious of technique, of the choreography and the many rehearsals.

One of the six bark paintings interwoven in the ceremony. The diamond pattern represents the fire which was brought by the great Baru and spread throughout the land.

Each plays a role and each role is studiously acted out. A grey bearded elder gazes in wonderment. A young brave heading a file of mourners stands respectfully to military attention.

The main file is led by a tall slim performer with a highly stylised walk. With his stomach contracted as though delt a heavy blow, chest hollowed, drooped shoulders thrust forward to dangle his arms like wings, he stalks forward with a jerking heel, toe and exaggerated knee action, like a wading brolga or jabiru.

A dance of communication, symbolising, perhaps the joining of two once hostile clans in mourning the death of their ancestor totem.

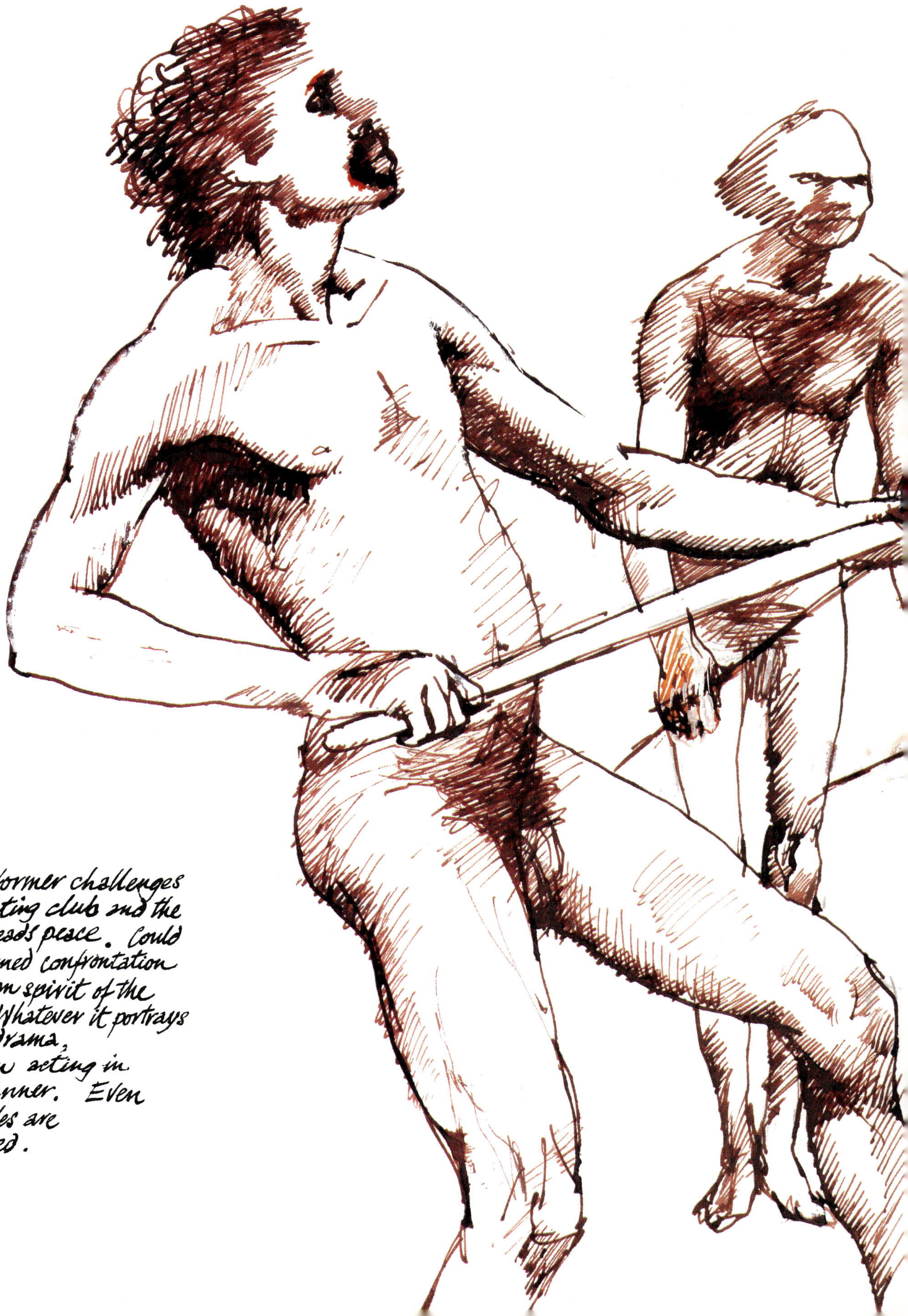

A leading performer challenges with his fighting club and the older man pleads peace. Could this be a mimed confrontation with the human spirit of the crocodile? Whatever it portrays this is high drama, Shakespearian acting in the grand manner. Even the minor roles are well rehearsed.

Each sequence of the drama climaxes on a dying note from the didjeridu; then the sticks clap it back to drone in the next act. Exhaling through vibrating lips, his Adam's apple and lower jaw moving up and down, the big man mouths words into the long tube; words of no particular meaning but vital to the continuity of different rhythmic patterns. Frequent breaths are snatched through the nose while air, stored in the puffed cheeks, is expelled down the tube to keep a continuous note sounding. In rapid alternation with the fundamental legato a high note is "spat" without disturbing the constant pitch. A highly skilled performance; but this is the home of the didjeridu.

Originally a product of North East Arnhem Land, known locally as a 'yiraki' or 'jiragi', this lugubrious woodwind has become popular across Australia's north from the Kimberleys to Cape York. It is simply a branch of a tree hollowed by termites. Its size, ranging from one to two metres and expanding conically from roughly 4 cms at the mouth end to 8 cms at the other, controls the tone.

With a dilly bag perched as a headdress and a biting bag clenched in his teeth a plump elder bends his knees and points urgently to the approaching crocodile. Behind him another old chap dangles his arms from drooped shoulders, his lion-like head expressing rapture. Two others in this group waiting at base like a reception committee, one with a biting bag, prod their spears into a pile of dry grass, soon to be touched off by Baru, bringer of fire.

Teeth defiantly clamped on a colourfully feathered biting bag, a lithe young warrior, armed with a decorated ceremonial club and a fist of spears, skips away from the group, his feet moving so swiftly in the dust and sand that he appears to glide above it. He dances solo close to the bark paintings of 'Baru' ritual designs. With high knee action he pounds his feet to the beat of clap-sticks and chanting, which is now pitched high above the deep drone of the didjeridu, the dust rising with the steadily increasing tempo.

A dancer in front and another to the side of the main body turn and cross in a series of step-hops then slide to one side with knees bent and open, feet sliding together, knees beating the rhythm.

From behind the group a warrior aims a spear high. Out in front a tall man raises a shovel-nosed spear then points it to the ground with the flourish of a drum major.

In deferential crouch all shuffle slowly, each man with bottom thrust out and arms falling loosely from drooped shoulders like a wallaby.

The files of dancers open and join together to form a U around the crocodile and its bearers; the ceremonial bark paintings are brought before the honoured ancestor for his approval.

A dancer approaches the totem, drops to the ground then shuffles on his knees back to the group. Another on knees cringes while offering a splendidly feathered biting bag which is placed between the fearsome teeth of the great Bäru.

Crouching like a music hall villain an actor creeps in from the side, casting exaggerated glances in all directions before touching a burning taper to the piles of yellow grass. All retreat in awe of the sudden flame then crane forward for a closer look. Pushing through the performers legs a man on his stomach smothers the flame, scrabbling sand with hands working like the flippers of a turtle covering her eggs.

Above the drone of the didjeridu and the clapping of sticks the volume of audience chanting and clapping swells as the tempo increases. With knees flexed the dancers stomp, knee high, foot parallel to the ground then pounded into the gritty sand to the steadily building pace of the rhythm — the vitality of pitch and pace generates a tingling excitement. Ears pound to the beat and the pressure of the crescendo is almost unbearable. Suddenly the action and sound are cut! The ears ring with the silence.

An elaborate
biting bag,
containing shells
and sacred
objects, is placed
between the gaping
jaws and the
death of this
awesome beast
is mourned
convincingly
by the women

The Museum team of pallbearers led by their Director, Dr. Colin Jack-Hinton, carry the great Ancestor Baru, a sacred dilly bag now clenched in its fearsome teeth, to the shade of a banyan tree closer to its final resting pad.

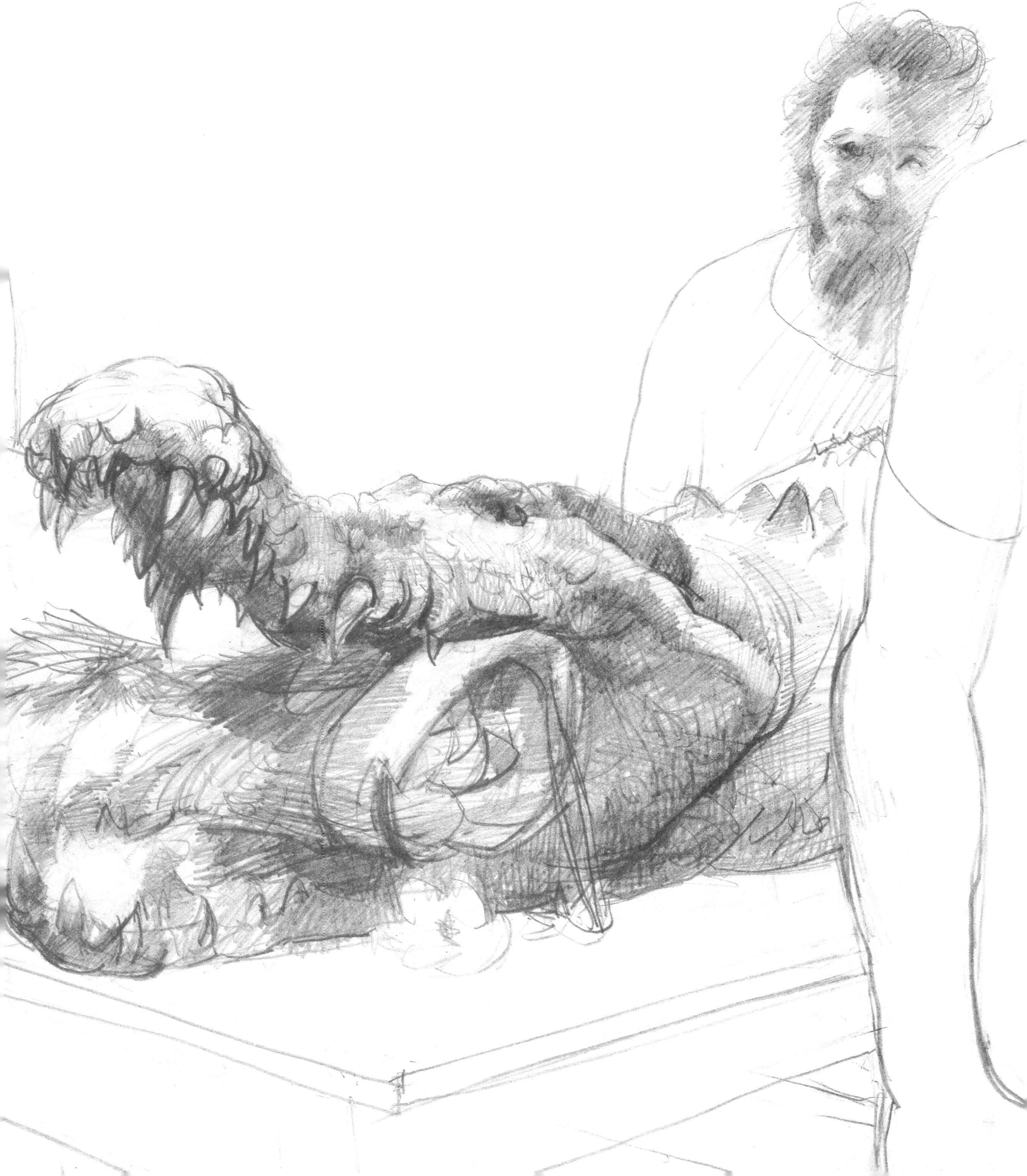

Most travelled of crocodiles Cuthbert, after five years in Darwin, continues in limbo as guest of NABALCO. Encased in the deified beast the spirit of Yunupingu the elder haunts the company's office in Gove. Cuthbert's final resting place will be Gulurruy's home to be built at Catalina Beach. Architects have measured him for entombment on a plinth of honour between living room and kitchen.

This gladdens Ian Archibald. Aware of tradition that artefacts made and sanctified for ceremony are no longer significant once the spirit of the deity has been satiated he had feared that his fine craftsmanship would be abandoned to return to nature.

The unique enshrinement of a mummified crocodile is a significant gesture expressing the merging of Aboriginal and European cultures; and Gulurruy's determination that his people will not forget Aboriginal lore will be celebrated in song cycle mourning the death of the crocodile.

Deep in the blood the past beats in all of us. This is specifically true among Aborigines. For more than 40,000 years this has been the strength of their culture — their continuity and survival.

For each in his house of sky clothing was unnecessary till less than 100 years ago when white folk imposed their shame. For this reason I have depicted them naked as they were, not degraded in cast off rags or as adult performers comical in diapers.

A concept of Arnhem Land with its 2000 million years of history is impossible to realise in painting. The written word helps contain space in time. It occured to me that sketches, both written and drawn together with paintings and archeological, anthropological, zoological and historical data could help me feel into the shadows of the ancient escarpment for the first abrupt edge of being.

Standing up to 2 metres, slightly taller than the male, the female emu leads in courtship dance. The male is available for sex each second year only. The female, which may lay twice in a season (breeding with separate males) abandons each clutch to her responsible mate for incubation and protection of the chicks till they mature at 2 years. They may live 40 years. Like other flightless birds which depend on ground speed the emu has only 3 toes; it runs up to 50 km/h.
Both sexes make a deep booming sound and loud guttural grunts, the female's harsh, the male's sharper.

Acknowledgements

I am grateful to many people for help in the publication of this book. Special thanks are due to the staff of the Museum of Arts and Sciences, Darwin. In particular I would like to thank Dr Colin Jack-Hinton, Director, Museums and Art Galleries of the Northern Territory; George Chaloupka, field anthropologist, Aboriginal rock art; Margaret West, Curator of Aboriginal Art and Material Culture; Ian Archibald, taxidermist. Thanks are also due to Nipper Kaparigi and George Mingum, traditional owners, Kakadu National Park; Dr Rhys Jones, Senior Fellow, Department of Prehistory, Research School of Pacific Studies, Australian National University, Canberra; and to individuals and collections housing examples of Aboriginal art from which the drawings have been interpreted: Aboriginal Artists Agency for permissions from the holders of design motifs; Museum of Victoria; Western Australian Art Gallery; Department of Anthropology, University of Western Australia; National Museum of Australia; Howard Morphy; and the Macleay Museum, University of Sydney.

ARNHEM LAND in the NORTH

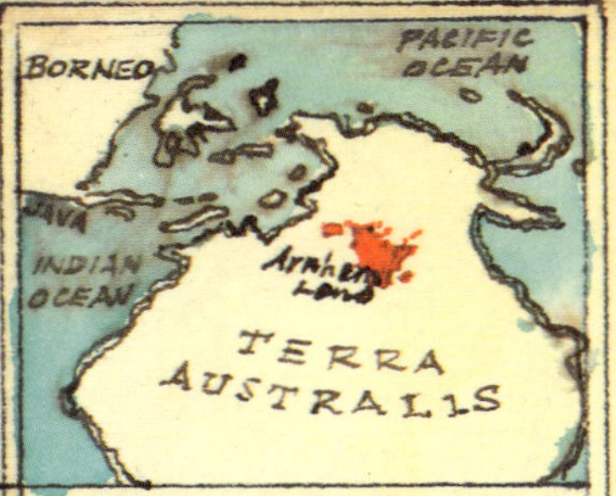

Land Mass of Australia and New Guinea at lowest sea levels of the Ice Age. Arnhem Land is inset.

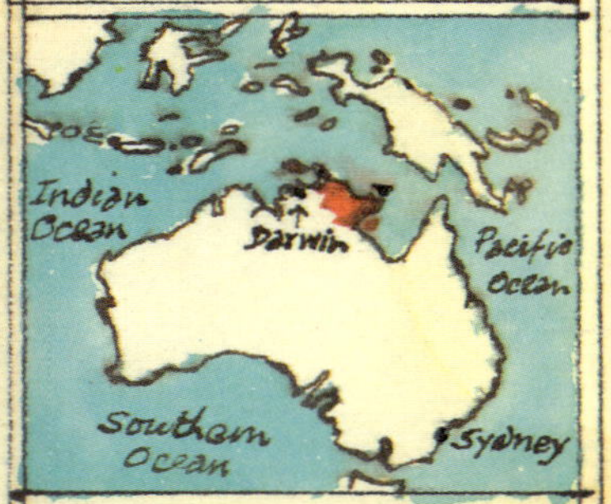

Darwin is equidistant from Singapore and Sydney and closer to the Equator than Jamaica or Fiji, Madras or Aden.

The Tropic of Capricorn is south of Arnhem Land. The Northern Territory is six times the area of the British Isles.